the art of
inspiration

an editor's guide to writing
POWERFUL, EFFECTIVE
inspirational & personal
development books

BRYNA RENÉ HAYNES

Published by Inspired Living Publishing, LLC.
P.O. Box 1149, Lakeville, MA 02347

ISBN-13: 978-0-9845006-6-6
ISBN-10: 0-9845006-6-9

Library of Congress Control Number:

www.InspiredLivingPublishing.com
(508) 265-7929

Cover and Layout Design: Bryna René Haynes

Editor: Bryna René Haynes & Matthew Haynes, www.TheHeartofWriting.com

Printed in the United States.

dedication

This book is dedicated to Matthew,
    without whom it would never have come to light.

writers are saying ...

"I've worked with Bryna since 2010, and when it comes to heart-centered, transformational editing, there's no one better. Her insights and authentic support will take your writing to the next level with love, and give you the confidence you need to share your work with the world."

- LINDA JOY, founder of *Aspire Magazine* & 7-time best-selling
publisher at Inspired Living Publishing

"*The Art of Inspiration* lives up to its title with a sublime balance of practical knowledge and heart. This book offers just what you need to write a moving and effective self-help book—one that truly holds the power of transformation. Editor Bryna Rene Haynes is at once wise, nurturing, inspiring and full of instruction and tips that will make a difference in your writing from the moment you start to apply them."

- LISA TENER, Book Coach, Silver Stevie Award Winner,
Mentor Coach of the Year 2014

"The most important thing you need to write a life-changing book is a fiery-hot passion for your topic. The second most important thing you need is the guidance of this book. I wish I'd had *The Art of Inspiration* while writing my first books—it would have made the process so much easier!"

- BONI LONNSBURRY, conscious creation expert, award-winning,
best-selling author of *Messages From Your Unseen Friends Vol. I* and
The Map: To Our Responsive Universe, Where Dreams Really Do Come True!

"Oh, how I could have used The *Art of Inspiration* prior to formulating my ideas and outline for Being Love. It would have saved me years of reworking my concept and thousands of dollars in developmental editing costs. What I love most is the way this book connected with me as a writer. I felt seen, heard and supported through the process of inspirational writing, as if I was talking with my best friend. Bryna's step-by-step approach is easy to follow and makes the daunting process of writing a book feel much more manageable. A must read for anyone considering writing a book especially an inspirational or self-help book!"

- DR. DEBRA L. REBLE, international best-selling author of
Being Love: How Loving Ourselves Creates Ripples of Transformation
in Our Relationships and The World

"*The Art of Inspiration* is Bryna René Haynes' gift to all storytellers and authors who want to use the written word to inspire others. I've personally used Bryna's approach as a chapter author for two (soon to be three) international best-selling books. As my editor, she awakened a richness in my writing that had previously lain dormant, waiting to come alive. This guide takes you through the exact process she uses with her private clients. Using Bryna's unique approach to writing allows every aspiring author to activate, arrange, and deliver personal development and inspirational books that serve the world like no others can."

- LAURA CLARK, the Soul Wise Living Mentor, international best-selling
coauthor of *Inspiration for a Woman's Soul: Cultivating Joy*, and *Inspiration for a*
Woman's Soul: Choosing Happiness

"If the thought of writing an inspirational or personal development book conjures visions of fighting your way to the top of Mount Everest, take a few deep breaths, and then immerse yourself in this book. Any adversity will soon give way to inspiration, creativity, excitement, and a knowing that you can bring your grandest vision to life."

- MICHAEL J. RUSS, founder of Zero Adversity™ Training

"I have gotten so many compliments over the past couple of years on my writing style, my authenticity and vulnerability in my writing. It hasn't always been this way. I've always been a writer; but I haven't always been one you could connect with. My writing was scientific, analytical, detached. Then I met Bryna René Haynes. She pushed me to tell my story and to tell it in such a way that women could relate to me. She pushed me to be more open, more vulnerable, more me in my writing. She asked me questions, she made me think about my own life experiences in a whole new way. She completely transformed my writing style. And I am forever grateful to and for her."

- DR. MARY E. PRITCHARD, BodyLove Expert, best-selling coauthor of
Inspiration for a Woman's Soul: Cultivating Joy, and
Inspiration for a Woman's Soul: Choosing Happiness

table of contents

PART 3 | POLISH AND REFINE

PART 4 | THE BIG REVEAL

the art of
inspiration

introduction

W hat does it mean to *inspire*?

> **Inspire:** /in'/*spī(ə)r/: *To fill (someone) with the urge or ability to do or feel something, especially to do something creative; to create (a feeling, especially a positive one) in a person.**

The word itself evokes a sense of lightness; a feeling that there are possibilities beyond our current worldview and experience. To inspire someone is to bestow upon them the gift of passion and a broader vision—one that will ultimately help them create a more positive experience for themselves and others.

At some point in our lives, we have all been blessed to receive inspiration—whether through a book, a movie, a conversation with a friend, an educational seminar, or a random magical moment. In some way, we can all relate to the feeling of being struck by that divine spark—the feeling of having a fire lit inside of us, of suddenly feeling full to the brim with ideas and possibilities.

When you undertake to create an inspirational book, your task is not only to strike the spark for your reader, but to lay the kindling for that divine fire so that the spark has someplace to land. Every piece of information you offer, every story you share, every truth you draw forth from the page, will serve as tinder for that transformational flame.

**Adapted from the definition listed at http://www.oxforddictionaries.com*

As many of us know from our childhood camping days, the fires that burn the longest and brightest are those laid with care and precision. Make the kindling too dense, or try to pile on too much heavy material at once, and the fire will go out. Spread things too sparsely, and it won't catch either. A solid foundation, plenty of breathing room, and your own "magic touch" are the keys to a roaring blaze.

Of course, writing a book is a wee bit more complex than building a campfire—but the analogy still holds. The spark is your purpose and vision, your reason for writing. The kindling is your narrative, the emotions and ideas you present, and the tools you give the reader. If well-organized and thoughtfully arranged, these components prepare the reader to receive the divine spark of inspiration with a wide-open mind and heart—and, more importantly, to know what to do with it when it comes.

My purpose in writing this manual is to assist you in this inspirational fire-building. In these pages, I offer up the knowledge I've gained in over a decade as a freelance editor, writer, and ghostwriter for authors in the inspirational, self-help, and personal development fields. Not only will I give you tools and tips for navigating the technical aspects of composition—like creating your outline, honing your stories, and completing your first, second, and third drafts—I will offer support for the unique emotional and intellectual challenges inherent in the creation process for books of this type.

Why am I sharing this knowledge with you? Because my "spark" is the belief that *everyone* has the potential to inspire others.

You picked up this book, which means that you have a spark, too. It is my honor and privilege to assist you in bringing your vision to life.

A BIT ABOUT MY APPROACH

Let me be frank: I'm not what you would call a "typical" editor.

My background is diverse, and my studies have included not only the art and practice of writing but also yoga, meditation, and various other self-inquiry modalities.

When I work with authors to create, refine, and deliver their books, I don't just correct their grammar and punctuation, or pronounce their writing "acceptable" or "unacceptable." Rather, I consider it my job to educate them about the writing process, and provide whatever assistance they require to write as their best and most inspiring selves. Often, this means working with them to overcome personal fears, emotional blocks, and other barriers that prevent them from accessing their authentic voice and message.

Therefore, in addition to practical tools, guidelines, and action steps, you will also find several "esoteric" components in this book, like self-inquiry questions, meditations, and my own observations about writers and their patterns. Not all of these items will resonate with you, but some will. Take what you need, and leave what doesn't serve you.

Another thing you should know about me is that I prefer questions to answers.

You know the old saying, "Give a man a fish, and he'll eat for a day. Teach a man to fish, and he'll eat for life." The same applies to writing. Yes, I could give you a formula to create The Best Inspirational Book Ever—but the capacity to write in an effective, engaging, *inspirational* manner cannot be gained by copying someone else's successful strategy. Rather, it comes from your ability to *ask the right questions,* and answer them in a way that invites continual improvement.

My teaching strategy is less about "right" and "wrong," and more about "why" and "how." I will never ask you to compare your work to that of other writers (a method I find detrimental in nearly every circumstance), and I have no desire to indoctrinate you into a branded formula. Right and wrong are subjective, and, in my experience, *there is no one formula that works for everyone.* You are an individual, and your book creation process will be as singular as you are.

It is my goal to walk beside you as you bring your book to life, and teach you to ask the questions that will lead you to the knowledge, skills, and self-understanding your book demands. These questions will act as guideposts along your own unique pathway of creation.

In other words, I will not only teach you how to write an inspirational book; I will teach you to *think, feel,* and *create* like an inspired writer.

THE EXPERT MYTH

One of the most common questions new writers ask me is, "Can I actually write about this? I'm not an expert!"

The idea that you need to be an expert to write a book has somehow taken hold of the collective consciousness and permeated every corner of non-fiction writing. But the Expert Myth is just that: a myth. You don't need a bunch of letters after your name to write an inspiring book. You don't need a formal education in your subject—or any formal education at all, for that matter. You simply need to know something your readers don't.

Have you noticed that the word "expert" is directly related to the word "experience"? Your *expertise* comes from your experience in your subject matter—whether formal or informal, deliberate or accidental.

If you have lived it, you can teach it.

So please, don't give up on your dreams of writing just because you don't have an advanced degree, or a following of tens of thousands of people. You would be doing the world a tremendous disservice. Just write what you know, authentically and passionately, and the people who need to learn from you will find you.

ENGAGING WITH YOUR PERSONAL PROCESS

You are standing on the brink of a transformational experience, one that will rock your world and open doors you can't even imagine from where you stand right now.

By taking this first step—by saying, "Yes, I can do this! I can write a book!"—you have set foot on a path of empowerment. Congratulations! But, you see, the spark really is only the first step. Once you start the writing process, you can expect to engage with your material in a visceral, immediate, and sometimes profoundly uncomfortable way. This journey will touch places in your soul that have never seen the light of day, and draw forth wisdom you didn't realize you possessed.

Through the seemingly simple act of putting words on paper, you will distill and purify your own ideas, and tap into the core of your own knowledge. You will be called upon to apply your teachings to your own life—just as you will eventually ask readers to do. And, with the help of the tools in this book, you will expand upon those things that serve you and your vision (through the channel of your book) and set aside, without regret or shame, those which do not.

There may also be transformational aspects to the creation process that fall outside the realm of your book's message. If you are willing, this journey will be an opportunity to face your fears about expressing your truth, committing to your message, and being *seen* in the world. For some, these emotional hurdles are the most challenging part of writing; recognizing this, I've endeavored to provide support in these areas as well.

Whether you are starting this book project as an experienced writer or a first-time author, my request of you is the same: remain open, curious, and teachable throughout this process. Not for my sake (although it is my deeply-held intention for you to create a brilliant, successful book with the assistance of this manual), but for your own. If you are willing to invite the unknown to sit beside you, if you are willing to allow yourself the space and compassion to grow through this work, you will be amazed at what comes through onto your pages.

Art is not a product of the hands, but a mirror of the soul. So let your soul shine through, trust yourself and this process, and let the sparks fly!

Welcome to *The Art of Inspiration.*

part 1

where to start

chapter 1

YOU ARE AN INSPIRATION

Your Purpose, Vision, and Practice

Imagine that you and I are meeting for coffee at your favorite café. When we sit down across from one another, I can see that you're excited.

"I have this *great* idea," you say. "I want to write an inspirational book."

"That's wonderful!" I respond. "I'm thrilled for you! But why an *inspirational* book?"

The way you answer that question will reveal a lot about your vision for this book, and your purpose in writing it.

You chose this path for a reason. Something inside you spoke up and said, "Yes! I can write a book!" More, you selected this manual to guide you in your writing journey. Those deceptively simple steps—committing to your goal and opening this book—have set you upon a path of empowerment, personal growth, and ultimately, inspiration.

You have something unique and momentous to share, and a spiritual imperative to bring it forth into the world. Your voice *matters*.

Take a moment to connect with that truth. Feel your excitement. Taste your anticipation. Then, lock this whole-body feeling into your cellular memory banks. *This* is the energy that will power you through the writing process, and infuse each page with the strength of your conviction, excitement, and vision.

And then, come back and meet me in the imaginary coffee shop, because before you start pounding out Chapter 1, there are a few things you will want to do, like:

- Write a Purpose Statement for your book.
- Choose a working title for your book.
- Establish your overall tone.
- Set your goals and create a writing plan.
- Create a solid outline (which we'll tackle in Chapter 2).

Besides, you haven't answered my question:

WHY AN INSPIRATIONAL BOOK?

Here are a few reasons why you might want to write a book.

- This philosophy/practice helped me in my life, and I want to share it.
- Many others out there are going through the same things I did, and I want to help them.
- I want to create a "calling card" for my client-centered or purpose-driven business.
- I want to establish myself as an expert in my field.
- I want to write a book that will interest a wide audience and potentially make a lot of money.

A book is a great way to share your story in a structured, deliberate way; reach fresh markets for your business; and gain credibility with those who don't know you personally, but who might be interested in what you offer. Plus, self-help and inspiration are hot markets right now, and they show no sign of slowing down—so if your goal is to write a best-seller, you might have a better shot in this category than in some others.

Nearly every story can be slanted as a "teaching story," and nearly every idea which reveals itself as the basis for an inspirational or self-help book can work in that context. Sometimes, though, it can take a little massaging to fit your material into the (albeit broad) definition of "inspirational" or "personal development."

Inspirational and self-help writing is all about the *angle*. For example, let's say you are a mental health therapist working with veterans to find new ways of coping with PTSD and battlefield trauma. A book about your methods will certainly be informative and illuminating—but will it be "self-help"? Will it be "inspirational"?

Well, that depends.

A book detailing your therapy methods could be directed at other professionals and people in your field—which would still fulfill your goal of being recognized as an expert—or it could be directed at veterans themselves, and offer advice and information that they can use, on their own, to improve their mental health and increase their happiness day-to-day. Only the second approach would categorize your book as a self-help or inspirational book.

"So," you may be asking, "What makes inspirational books different from other non-fiction books?"

Inspirational, self-help, and personal development books:

- Answer a question, solve a problem, or create a new level of understanding.

- Have an educative component that is obviously stated and thoroughly explored in the text.

- Have a clear and uplifting message which empowers readers to create positive change in their lives.

- Are primarily focused on readers and the message(s) they are receiving from the text, rather than the story hero/heroine, an action-based plot, or the narrator

So, if you want to share your opinion or expertise, but not necessarily "teach" readers what to do with the lessons contained therein—or if your story is more of a juicy exposé than an inspirational journey—you may be better off in another genre.

Also, if you're writing your book to make a pile of money (and who doesn't want to make a pile of money?) you will want to cultivate some additional motivation beyond simply being the next Eckhart Tolle or Dr. Wayne Dyer—not because it is wrong to want your book to succeed, or even for success to be your primary motivation, but because readers can sense passion and purpose on the page. If your book feels trite and formulaic, or doesn't spark that proverbial "lightbulb moment" for your readers, it will fall flat. Period, end of story.

If you feel unsteady in any of these areas—story material, angle, or your own motivation—take some time to sink into your purpose and vision. Feel your way through your ideas, and ask for guidance from your muse, your friends, or your higher power. Sometimes you just need a little shift in perspective for everything to click into place.

YOUR MESSAGE: THE HEART OF YOUR BOOK

Now that you are clear about *why* you want to write an inspirational book (as opposed to just a regular old book), it's time to tune in to your book's *message*.

Every book has its own message and energy, and yours will, too.

Regardless of how many other books exist on your chosen subject, there is something about your message and delivery that is unique, and will speak to readers in a way no other book can. The perspective you bring through your own life experience, your personal stories, the tone and cadence of your writing voice, the themes you choose to explore, and the way in which you engage with those themes; all of these will differentiate you from other authors in the field.

However, in order to share this uniqueness with your readers, you need to inspire them to pick up your book in the first place.

How do you do that? You hook them with your *message*.

Throughout the writing process, your message—as expressed in the Purpose Statement you'll write in the next section—will be your North Star, your guiding light, the standard against which all things for your book are measured. It will help you craft your outline. It will help you gauge what material to include in your book, and what to save for another project. And finally, it will be your "elevator pitch," the concise and focused description you will use when speaking about your book to others, or pitching it to an agent or publisher.

Your Purpose Statement

Your Purpose Statement is a crystal-clear encapsulation of your message, intentions, subject matter, and target audience.

To begin creating your Purpose Statement, ask yourself these six Purpose Questions:

- What is the overall message of my book?
- What are the themes I intend to use in my book?
- Who is my ideal reader?
- What question(s) does my subject matter pose and answer, and what problem(s) does it solve for my readers and/or society as a whole?
- What can readers expect to learn from my book, and why do they need to learn it?
- Why am I the perfect person to write this book?

It may seem simple at first glance, but creating your Purpose Statement can be one of the most challenging parts of the whole writing process. Why? Because it requires you to get extremely clear about your subject and your relationship to it. If you came to this process with a vague idea like, "I'm going to write a book about positivity!" the creation of your Purpose Statement will help you narrow your field of vision, and hone in on which aspects of "positive" you really want to teach, and to whom.

To further assist you in this process, let's look at each of the above questions in more detail.

What is the overall message of my book?

Your overall message is the "empowerment piece" of your book— the help or assistance that you are offering your readers, and the reason they will pick your book off the shelf.

For example, if you are writing a book about creating more love in your current relationships, your overall message will be something like, "You can find more love in all of your relationships, right now!"

Seems pretty obvious, right? It certainly can be. But once you are clear about your message, look carefully at the words you have chosen, and be sure that they feel natural and authentic to you, and that they fit the energy and tone you want to convey. To expound on the above example: "You *can* find more love in your relationships, no matter how challenging they are right now," is a very different message than, "Your relationships don't have to suck!" One is soft, one is snarky. Both could very easily work—as long as the tone of the message is reflected throughout your book.

If you aren't sure what your overall message is, tune into your personal gifts. What problems do you solve for your friends, clients, and coworkers every day? What kinds of advice do people consistently ask you for? Especially if you're a business owner using your book to establish your expert status, you will want your book's overall message to directly reflect, support, and enhance the work you do in the world.

What are the themes used in the book?

Your themes are the specific messages, angles, and focal points which will help you individualize your overall message and connect to your target audience.

For example, a book about positivity might focus on the themes of positivity in relationships, positivity at work, or positivity in the face of ill health. Your themes will be reflected in the stories and examples you choose during the writing process to illustrate and support your overall message.

Try to stick to one or two main themes. If you try to explore too many different themes in your book, you will overwhelm your readers and actually dilute your message.

Finally, your themes can also tell you a lot about your target audience—which, of course, is the next item on our list.

Who is my ideal reader?

Please don't say "everyone!"Not because you can't write a book that will benefit a diverse or even a worldwide audience, but because such a broad answer will not help you in your creation process.

Your book is essentially a conversation with your ideal reader. As the narrator, it's your responsibility to show that person the path to the solution s/he desires.

Sometimes, your book concept will identify your ideal reader for you, with almost no effort on your part. For example, if you are writing a guidebook for parents of children with Oppositional Defiant Disorder, your audience is pretty well-defined. But what do you do when your book has a broader, more universal message?

If you aren't sure who your ideal reader is, ask yourself, "Whose life do I want to change, and how? What does that person look and sound like? What does s/he do for work? What is his/her family life like?" Be as specific as you can.

For example, if your book is about dealing with abandonment, you could say, "This book is for every person who has ever felt alone and abandoned." But that doesn't give you a clear picture of your ideal reader—so what if you asked, "Alone and abandoned in what way? By their parents? By society? By a lover?" Your answer will give you a clue about the person for whom you are really writing.

What question(s) does my subject matter pose and answer, and what problem(s) does it solve for my readers and/or society as a whole?

If your readers had all the answers, they wouldn't need your book!

Every inspirational or self-help book asks a question. If written with consistent attention to the overall message and themes, it answers that question as well—at least, as much as humanly possible.

Take a moment to reflect on the questions that your overall message poses to your audience. For example, my overall message for this book is, "There is an art to writing inspirational and self-help books which anyone can implement to create powerful, effective written work." Therefore, the question posed by this book is, "How do I (the reader) write a powerful, effective inspirational or self-help book?"

Once I identified the overall question, I knew exactly what my book needed to include in order to answer that question. As I wrote and refined my chapters, I asked myself, "Is this information necessary to help my readers create powerful, effective inspirational books?" If the answer was no, I knew that the material did not belong in my book.

Of course, my subject matter is pretty clear-cut. What happens when the subject is more fluid?

There are a million ways to approach any subject—and there is probably more than one right way for you, so don't get too caught up in finding the "perfect" angle. Instead, ask yourself questions like, "When I first started exploring this material, what questions did I have?" (Chances are, they were something along the lines of, "How will this help me?" and "What will I get out of this?") You could also ask, "What were my biggest struggles or learning curves in this area of my life?" or "What was the belief about this subject that I struggled most to change?"

If you aren't sure how to frame the questions your book addresses, ask your friends and colleagues for help. What information would they ideally receive from a book on your chosen subject? What questions do they want answered, and what positive changes do they want to create?

What can readers expect to learn from my book, and why do they need to learn it?

You answered part of this question in the previous section: what readers can expect to learn is the answer to the book's overall question. Now, let's get more specific, and ask why.

For example, if your book answers the question, "How can I cease my negative self-talk forever?" you will also want to identify all the reasons that someone would want to stop their negative self-talk.

This part may seem like a no-brainer, but don't skip it. When you list all the reasons someone might want to implement the change you are suggesting, or follow the program you are creating, you are actually developing "talking points" for use throughout your book, as well as gaining clarity for your book's overall focus and direction.

Why am I the perfect person to write this book?

Don't go all modest on me! Write down all the reasons why you are perfect to write this book, why you are uniquely qualified to speak to your chosen audience on your subject matter, and why no one else could possibly offer what you do. Write the stellar introduction you would want to hear Matt Lauer read the first time you appear on *The Today Show.*

List all the ways in which you have interacted with your chosen subject over time. List the life experiences that have shaped your viewpoint and sharpened your understanding. List your credentials (academic and otherwise) if they are applicable. Throw in a bit more about your motivations, and your passion for this subject matter. Then, condense your "brag statements" into a few sentences that tell readers why you really are the perfect person to impart this information.

If you are struggling with this process, ask a trusted friend or colleague for help. It is always an enlightening experience to read about yourself from someone else's perspective, and the descriptive words your helper chooses might be more accurate, and more powerful, than the ones you chose for yourself.

Write Your Purpose Statement

Sit with the Purpose Questions for as long as it takes for you to get clear on each element. If you hit points of resistance, or feel unsteady, try answering all of the questions again from another angle. Switch up your themes and message. Play with reader outcomes. Do this over and over until you feel really connected to your purpose.

Then, write your Purpose Statement.

Your Purpose Statement will include all of the information you outlined in the Six Purpose Questions, along with your personal desire around the outcome (which you explored in the previous section). It is an energetic declaration, an encapsulation of your vision, and a reference point for your entire creation process.

There are as many ways to write a Purpose Statement as there are writers! No matter how you choose to write yours, remember that clarity is the most important feature of a Purpose Statement. Keep it short and sweet—no more than two or three sentences, and ideally just one.

Here's a template you can use to get started. But please, don't just fill in the blanks! Really work with your Purpose Statement to be sure it includes every element of your vision, message, intention, and desired reader outcome.

> *My purpose in writing this book is to [action word] [audience] to [action related to your teaching or expertise], [secondary action], and [result].*

Here's the Purpose Statement I created for this book.

> *My purpose in writing this book is to codify the knowledge I've gained in over a decade as an editor, and empower writers of all experience levels to create powerful inspirational/self-help books which deliver their positive messages to a global audience.*

Your Purpose Statement can (and probably will) change a bit during the writing process as you explore your themes and material. Each time you sense a shift in your overall mission, themes, or target readership, come back to the drawing board, and rewrite your Purpose Statement to reflect these changes. This process will keep you in touch with the "heart" of your work, and serve as a touchstone when the time comes to edit and revise your content.

CHOOSE A WORKING TITLE FOR YOUR BOOK

You may be wondering, "Why would I choose my title *after* writing my Purpose Statement?"

Well, because your book title is one of three key components (along with your cover and back cover text) that will entice readers to pick up your book. Now that you are crystal-clear about your purpose and intention, you are ready to create a stunning, memorable working title that perfectly encapsulates the energy and purpose of your book— a title you can get excited about.

On the flip side, you might also be wondering why you should choose a title *before* you start writing. What if your book evolves into something different? What if your themes change? Well, as the section title states, you are not choosing your "forever title"; you are choosing a *working title*—the title you will be working with as you write and edit your book.

A working title can help you visualize your book as a completed product, and anchor the book concept in your mind. It also gives you a way to refer to your book when you share it with other people.

What Your Title Does

A book title does three things. It grabs a reader's interest; it gives a clue as to what's in the book (including overall message and tone); and, because this is an inspirational book, it *makes a promise to the reader.*

The last is the most important. When readers are aware of the possible result of reading your book before they even open the cover, they are more likely to perceive its value. Look at some of the most successful titles in the genre: their promises are loud and clear. (This is not to say that you can't be successful with an ambiguous title; however, you will need to make up for it with a great subtitle.)

A great inspiration/self-help book title should be:

- **Short.** A title of less than seven words is ideal. Remember, this title will be used in internet searches, as a URL, and in print, online, and social media.

- **Easy to remember.** When someone hears good things about your book, they will probably look it up—but not if they can't recall the title.

- **Easy to say.** Many readers will hear about your book through word-of-mouth. Be sure your promoters aren't going to get tongue-tied!

- **Original.** Meaning, it hasn't been used as a book title before—at least in your target genre. (Book titles, like slogans, are not protected under copyright law, but if your title has been used before, be sure that your subtitle is clear and precise, so readers don't get confused.)

- **A clear statement about the book's contents.** "Mystery" titles, or titles pulled from a single line of the book, might work well for fiction or memoir, but readers of inspirational books want to know exactly what they're getting. If your title is catchy but ambiguous, be sure to shore it up with a great subtitle.

Your title might also do one (or more) of the following:

- Identify a need (*Healing ___, Letting Go of ___, Overcoming ___*).

- Offer a solution (*How to* ___, *Three steps to* ___).
- Utilize a standard, recognized format (*The* ___ *Workbook*).
- Showcase your trademarked words or phrases.
- Offer a call to action.

Finally, your book title should speak to your ideal readers and match your Purpose Statement in tone, content, and intended result.

Choose Your Subtitle

If your book title is the hook, your subtitle is the line that will reel in your readers.

The subtitle explains, clarifies, or expands on your book title. This is where you will state your promises to your readers, give additional clues as to the subject and content of your book, and place keywords or "trigger words" that speak to readers in your genre.

Your subtitle will probably evolve out of your overall message (which you identified while creating your Purpose Statement) but will also be more succinct. Use only as many words as you need to make the subject and promise of your book clear. Be sure to choose descriptive words that really fit your message, and reflect your chosen tone, themes, and angle.

Here are some possible formats for your subtitle:

- How [what you are teaching] can [create this result]. *Ex: How Honoring Yourself Can Save Your Relationship*
- Reflections on [subject matter]. *Ex: Reflections on Biblical Prophecies*
- One [person's] [experience, journey] with [subject]. *Ex: One Woman's Journey from Invisible to Inspirational*

- A guide for [ideal readers] who want to [desired action]. *Ex: A Guide for Yoga Practitioners Who Want to Grow Beyond Tradition*
- [Action prompt] and [result-oriented action], [timeline]. *Ex: Ditch The Excuses and Create Your Business in 30 Days!*

What To Do With The "Divine Title Download"

Maybe you skipped over the last three sections because you experienced a case of Divine Book Title Download. (See, I know how you roll!)

Sometimes, when you start thinking about your book, a title will just flash into your head. It happened to me with this book: all of a sudden, I saw the title, the cover, the layout … everything. (That was how I knew I had to write it!)

Quite often, that initial flash of inspiration is totally on target. But sometimes, when you really sit down to explore your purpose and vision for your book, the title with which you were so enamored can start to feel a little … off.

When that happens, don't force things. Instead, set aside your attachment, and ask yourself these questions:

- *Can I adjust this title* to align it with my purpose?
- *Will a targeted subtitle add enough clarity and focus* to bring this title in line with my purpose?
- *Do I need to choose a more appropriate title*, and save this one for another book?

If you need to choose a new title, don't let it get you down. Trust me, there's plenty more inspiration where that came from!

More Helpful Hints For Title Creation

- *Choose the descriptive words in your title and subtitle carefully.* I can't say this enough. One great word is better than ten clichés.

- *Make a long list of prospective titles.* Write down anything that comes into your mind. Then, create a "short list" from your brainstorming session. Your ideal title might be in that short list, or it might be a combination of several of your "finalists."

- *Ask for feedback.* Based solely on title, would your friends/family/colleagues buy your book? A quick verbal or e-mail survey asking for input on your short list can be quite enlightening.

- *Do your research.* Browse the shelves at your local bookstore, or do a search online. What books in your genre speak to you? What titles do you find catchy, and which boring? What makes a title stand out to you?

- *Look online for inspiration.* There are hundreds of articles and blogs about what makes a book title great—and everyone has their own opinion. See what resonates, and play around.

Finally, remember that this is a *working title.* You can change or upgrade it at any time. As you write, your ideas about what needs to be in the book may change. You may discover a whole new line of thought that hadn't occurred to you before. If that happens, your Purpose Statement and book title will certainly need to evolve with your content.

But, in the meantime …

Inspiring Ways To Put Your Working Title To Work

- *Create a mock-up of your book cover* (or have an artistic friend do it for you). Post this where can see it as you write, and visualize your book as complete.

- *Replace the #1 slot on the latest best-seller list with your own book title,* and hang it in a spot you see every day. Imagine what it will feel like when your book is out there in the world, and readers are eating it up.

- *Share your book title on social media,* like this: "Great news! [My working title] will be here next year, so keep your eyes peeled!" (Note: If the thought of announcing your project makes you panic, there's no need to do it!)

- *Write a first draft of your back cover text using your Purpose Statement as a baseline.* You will write your actual back cover text in Chapter 7—but for now, use this as an exercise to expand on your intention for the book. What do you want prospective readers to know? What about your book will make them want to read and recommend it?

- *Write a press release or article about your book,* focusing on the ways in which it will help your target audience and why it is a masterful addition to your genre. Re-read it whenever you need inspiration. (Bonus: you can also use this as a template for a real press release once your book is done!)

ESTABLISH YOUR OVERALL TONE

Now that you have your Purpose Statement and working title, it's time to set your intention for the overall tone of your book.

What Is "tone," exactly?

Well, as the old saying goes, "It's not what you say; it's how you say it." Tone is the way you express your *attitude and energy* in your writing. It shows up in your word choices, the examples you choose to illustrate your teaching points, and the angles from which you choose to approach your subject matter.

Your overall tone could be humorous or serious, sarcastic or light-hearted, academic or emotional, soft or pointed. It might be conversational or formal. It might be action-oriented or reflective. It might be conceptually lofty or pragmatic and logical.

Any of these tones could potentially be applied in an inspirational or self-help book, regardless of its subject matter. (Yes, you really could write a sarcastic or humorous self-help book—and if you did it right, it could even be effective.)

How do I choose the right tone?

Your Purpose Statement holds many clues about who your readers are, what they need, and what kind of help you are offering. Your working title (and your likes and dislikes for the titles you researched) hold further information about the overall tone you gravitate toward.

When working to identify an appropriate tone, award-winning book coach Lisa Tener instructs her clients to pinpoint what others love about their communication style. She says, "Think about why people are attracted to you. What do your friends and clients like most about your personality? Those are the things you should bring out in your tone. For example, if your clients love your nurturing energy, make sure that comes through in your book. If your writing is too dry, or too formal, they won't feel that connection."

The right tone for you will always be the one that is most authentic—the one that feels like an extension of your daily communication style. That is not to say that you can't shape your writing to fit the needs of the book—but if you are not a naturally sarcastic person, you might have to work a little harder to keep that black humor from falling flat.

My rule is: if you have to try too hard to create a tone, it is not the one you should be using.

If you're not sure what your natural tone is, read some of your written pieces aloud, or go back to old journals. See what jumps out at you about your own personal style.

Once you have identified your natural tone, put some descriptive words around it. (See some potential tone descriptions above.) Can you settle comfortably into the parameters your tone sets for your writing?

Next, compare your chosen tone to your Purpose Statement and working title. Are they compatible? Do the working title and subtitle give a clue as to the tone of the book? Does your Purpose Statement reflect the energy and tone that feels natural to you?

When these pieces are in alignment, you should have a solid "feeling" about your book and the energy you want to bring to it.

Take a moment to answer the following questions:

- I want my book to communicate ___ to readers.
- I want to communicate this information in a ___ way.
- I want my book to make readers feel ___.
- The overall energy of my book is ___.

"But why," you might ask, "do I need to identify and label my tone, if it's how I write naturally?"

Setting parameters at this early stage is a good idea because your tone will fluctuate—sometimes wildly—over the course of a large writing project. It will change depending on your mood, the books you're currently reading, and your overall confidence level. If you are unclear about your tone (and the intention behind it), your book may end up feeling a bit … schizophrenic.

Imagine that you have just called your best friend after a hard day. You are excited to speak to her, because she's a pretty chill lady, and you can always rely on her sweet, gentle voice to soothe your jangled nerves.

However, when she picks up the phone, the first thing she says is, "Yeah? Whaddaya want?"

At this point, you are probably confused. Why is she speaking in Brooklynese instead of her usual Texas twang?

Now, imagine that, as the conversation goes on, your friend (who is normally the most loving person you know) launches into a diatribe about how people who call her out of the blue really tick her off, and how she's tired of being everyone else's emotional landfill. More, she becomes angry when you don't immediately agree with her.

If that happened, you would probably hang up the phone a little shaken, thinking, "What the heck was that about? What has that crazy lady done with my best friend?" Next time you called (making sure to text first, to give her fair warning), you would probably feel guarded, mistrustful, and unsupported—and it would take several conversations for your friend to win your trust again.

A drastic shift in tone will shock your readers in precisely the same way.

A book which is consistent in tone flows feels stable and supportive to readers. Think about your favorite inspirational book, the one you always refer to when life pushes you around. No matter which page in the book you open to, you feel like the author is right there, coaching you through your process. This energetic "availability" is a result, at least in part, of steadiness of tone. When things are topsy-turvy for your readers, or they are in the middle of a learning curve, your book will provide steady ground—a place where they can return again and again to gain clarity, reassess, and prepare to move forward again.

Later, when you are revising, you can refer to the parameters you set in this section to determine whether a particular piece of material actually belongs in your book. If something you have written feels out of place (like potty humor in a serious book, or a very sad story in a humorous book), you can use your knowledge of tone to adjust it so it feels consistent—or at least create some context for it, so it doesn't sideswipe your readers.

SET YOUR GOALS AND CREATE A WRITING PLAN

I know there are coaches out there who say, "You can write and publish your book in twenty-one days!" And while that may be the case for some, I personally do not advise that approach.

"Why not?" you ask. "Why shouldn't I write my book and get it out there as quickly as possible?"

Imagine that you are standing on a beautiful path in your favorite part of the world. You could sprint down this path, and reach its end in record time—but what new experiences and ideas would you fly past in your dash to the finish? What beautiful vistas would you miss?

Your first and second drafts are your chance to fully explore your subject matter within the intentional boundaries you have established in this chapter. This process of exploration is unique for every writer, and is subject to all of the Universal Laws by which we live—including divine timing.

The boundaries of your Purpose Statement, tone, intentions, and outline are what create your path, and keep your feet grounded on it as you move forward. Without them, you might end up lost in the woods, running in circles, or even walking backward. But there are places on your path that will beckon you to sit awhile, and engage with them on a soul-deep level—just as there are stretches of open road that will call you to run.

"So," you ask, "If I allow myself this time for exploration, how long *should* it take me to write my book?"

For most people, I recommend allowing six to nine months (or more) to nurture a manuscript from purpose statement to final, self-edited draft—but that's only a recommendation. The real answer is, it will take as long as it takes.

Now, this doesn't mean that you shouldn't set goals for yourself. It only means that those goals should be reasonable for you, and support you to create your best possible material.

To that end, I encourage you to set *practice-based intentions* rather than *time- or output-based goals*.

A practice-based intention is exactly what it sounds like: an intention to engage with your writing practice. And writing *is* a practice, just like meditation, yoga, or T'ai Chi. Regardless of your starting point or level of experience, you will get the most out of your practice if you show up for it on a regular basis, and treat it as an evolving expression of your personal energy rather than a fixed skill set that you can drop and pick up again at will.

Practice-based intentions, in addition to building a closer relationship between you and your writing, also free you from the feeling that you "need to" meet certain milestones during your writing sessions. Especially when you are working on your first draft, it is vital to allow space for free writing, brainstorming, exploring tangents—and, above all, making mistakes. If you are always thinking, "I *need to* get this chapter done this week," your creative process will be compromised. (We'll talk more about free writing and first drafts in Chapter 3.)

Set Your Practice-Based Intention

To set your intention, first decide how great a priority your writing time is to you.

Before you say, "It's my highest priority," stop. Think about what it would *really* look like if you dropped everything in order to write.

I know, we've been conditioned to think that, as writers, putting words on paper must be our sole priority. Right now, you're probably picturing a "real writer"—someone totally lost in a private vision, tongue pinched between teeth, hair dirty and disheveled, typing furiously at 3:00 a.m. with three empty coffee mugs and an overflowing ashtray for company.

But here's the truth: writing should *never* be your highest priority, unless you want the rest of your life to turn into a hot mess.

If you are serious about your book and your message, writing should be a *very high* priority, but should always come second to your self-care and your most important relationships. (Notice I didn't say that it should come second to your job. That's for you to decide.)

Your practice-based intention should reflect your priorities and honor your schedule, and yet be rigorous enough to keep you moving steadily toward your goal of completing your book.

Like the rest of life, your writing practice is all about balance. If you set your sights on an unreasonable target, or allow your writing to deplete you, cause you stress, or undermine your relationships, you will very soon run out of creative juice. On the flip side, if everything in your life is a greater priority than your writing, your book will never get written.

Here are some questions to ask yourself when setting practice-based intentions for your book project.

- How many days per week do I want to write?
- What is the maximum amount of time I can reasonably allow per writing session?
- What is the minimum amount of time I require to be productive during a writing session?
- Do I have any major events, vacations, or other projects coming up that will require an adjustment to my writing time?
- Can I adjust my schedule to open up more writing time (i.e., watch less TV, shorten my lunch break at work)?
- Can I move or eliminate nonessential commitments to free up writing time?

Note, in the second question, the presence of the word "reasonably." If your Thursdays are packed full of family activities and you barely have time to make dinner or take a shower, Thursdays are probably not the best days to try to schedule productive writing time. Be gentle with yourself—and schedule an extra hour of writing time on Sunday instead, when your mother is around to watch the kids.

For most people, a great practice-based intention is, "I will work on my book for an hour every day this week."

Nearly everyone can spare an hour a day for a book project—even if that hour needs to be broken up into two or three shorter segments to accommodate family and work schedules. Most importantly, an intention like this will get you to your desk every single day, and prompt you to engage with your material for an hour, which is really half the battle in any writer's process.

Once you know how much time per day and week you will spend writing, put your writing times in your calendar. Make writing a daily ritual, and try not to miss your sessions. (If you can spend more time writing on Monday, great—but don't skip Tuesday as a reward!) Turn off your cell phone. Ask your family not to interrupt. Create sacred space for your practice with a short ritual or meditation. Do whatever it takes to get present to your process.

"But," you ask, "what about the days when I don't feel like writing?"

Don't put it off—write anyway! Even if you sit at your computer and type "I have no idea what to write" over and over again, you will still have honored your practice for the day. You can also devote your writing practice time to research, organization of supplemental materials, or brainstorming exercises, as long as they are directly related to your book.

You can't expect yourself to be "on" with your writing every single day—but you *can* expect yourself to show up to your writing in the same way you show up for your job, or your family, or anything else that is important to you. Some days, it will feel grudging; sometimes, you will even be angry about it. It doesn't matter. All that matters is that you honor your commitment to show up.

Now that you have scheduled your writing time for the foreseeable future, you can set goals around other aspects of your book project, like research, interviews, and story materials.

Here are five questions to ask about your supplemental materials:

- Does my book concept require research of facts, statistics, or studies?

- Do I have research of my own which needs to be organized, studied, or summarized?

- Does my book concept require, or would it benefit from, interviews (with experts or lay people or both), testimonials, or quotes?

- Does my book concept require me to obtain permission or waivers from clients, friends, or family in order to use their stories?

- Do any of the above need to be completed before I can start writing?

Sometimes, the answer to all of the above questions is, "I have absolutely no idea."

That's fine. The needs of your book will become clear as you complete your outline and first draft, and you can revisit this intention-setting process at that point. But if you know from the outset that your book will require research, interviews, or testimonials, it is helpful to set some intentions around completing those in a timely manner.

For example, you might set a date by which you intend to have all requests for interviews e-mailed, or all phone calls made. Or, you might schedule time every week for the next month to sort through your research and records and pull out relevant information. This can be done simultaneously with your writing process, or it can be done prior; it all depends on your intentions, the hours you can reasonably commit, and whether you need these materials before you start writing your first draft.

All in all, the intention-setting process creates a sense of accountability to your own vision. If you need additional reinforcement and feel comfortable asking for help, share your intentions with friends or colleagues, and invite them to be accountability partners.

When To Set Time-Based Goals

After examining your practice-based intentions and other pre-writing tasks (like interviewing), you might choose to set a reasonable, flexible time-based goal. However, I would only advise this if you:

- Have an easier time prioritizing tasks when you have a firm timeline.
- Do your best work under pressure.
- Have an external factor which necessitates the completion of your book by a certain date (such as a publisher's deadline, a major event where you can sell your book, or a product launch).

If none of the above apply, do *not set a time-based goal.* Just stick with your practice-based intention, and allow your book to evolve organically.

If the third point above applies to you, but you tend to get nervous under pressure, ask yourself how you can adjust your practice-based intentions to meet your timeline without a lot of worry and stress. Nothing kills creativity faster than anxiety and negative self-talk, so don't create a situation that invites those energies!

MOVING FORWARD

Great work! You have taken your first solid steps to establish the energetic and intentional foundation for your inspirational book.

Congratulate yourself for taking the time to get in touch with your vision and purpose for this project, and for setting the intentions which will keep you engaged and accountable through your creation process.

Now, it's time to create the framework that will support, direct, and give structure to your book:

It's time to write your outline!

chapter 2

THE ALL-IMPORTANT OUTLINE

Establish a Structure That Serves Your Book

Yes, I know. Outlining. Ugh.

For a long time, every time I wrote an outline, I was transported back to eighth-grade English class—which, although English was my favorite subject, and Mrs. Leary my favorite teacher, still wasn't the most pleasant of memoryscapes. My whole body would get tight with frustration, and I'd think to myself, "I know what I want to write! Why can't I just write it, already?"

These days, though, I love to outline, and definitely encourage anyone who has had a love-hate relationship with the outline in the past to give it another try. Why? Because there is no better tool than an outline to help you determine what your book really needs.

Why Is An Outline Important?

- *It gives you clarity* about the questions—both overall and specific—that your book asks and answers
- *It organizes your information* so that your book progresses logically from start to finish.
- *It helps you think critically* about your topic and angle
- *It helps you discern what really belongs* in your book.

A well-thought-out outline can also:

- *Remind you about what you actually know.* If you just sit down and start writing, many of the relevant points you could make will simply slip your mind. Outlining helps you identify everything you want to say.

- *Break your writing down into manageable chunks.* It can be daunting to think about writing something as long as a book or e-book. An outline has the effect of breaking up your topic into manageable bites that you can work on one at a time.

- *Help you stay on track.* Have you ever had a piece of writing start off as one thing and morph into something completely different? (I once had an article on the *Yoga Sutras* turn into a discourse on how yoga is taught in America. Not even close to where I started!) Sometimes, books change direction, and that's fine—but you don't want it to happen by accident.

- *It saves time in the editing stage.* If you create a solid outline, you will almost certainly have to do less revising later, because your topic, tone, and purpose will be consistent throughout.

WHAT IS AN OUTLINE?

An outline is an ordered list of topics, talking points, and other materials you wish to include in your book. The information is organized in the order of presentation, and categorized into chapters, subchapters, sections, and subsections.

That's it—just a list. Nothing to be afraid of.

An outline can take any form you like. Some writers work well from a simple bullet-point list, while others prefer to map out every detail before they start writing.

Personally, I like to create bullet-point lists under my chapter headers, which I can then cut and paste in the order that makes the most sense for the topic, tone, and purpose of the book. Some people prefer to write their outlines longhand, and only commit them to a screen once their brainstorm has blown itself out. Book coach Lisa Tener prompts participants in her writing program to write each topic on an index card, and then play with their order on a desk or corkboard where they can easily swap them around.

As long as whatever method you choose helps you to solidify the flow of content in your piece, it is a valid outlining technique.

Every book has its own structural imperatives. However, when your outline is complete, you should be able to clearly identify both the overall question asked by your book, and the process by which readers will create the outcome promised by your title.

Every book will do this differently, but no matter what, these two components *must* be present in order for your book's message to be effective.

"Okay," you may be saying to yourself. "That's all pretty self-explanatory. But how do I decide what actually goes into my outline?"

You start by creating an *Information Delivery System.*

OUTLINING STEP #1
YOUR INFORMATION DELIVERY SYSTEM

By the time you have come this far in conceptualizing your book, you will probably have some idea of the particular topics you want to address—but how do you determine what goes where, and which ideas take priority?

The best way to determine the overall flow and shape of your book is to look at your book's core questions, and then develop a system for presenting each vital piece of information to your readers.

When you wrote your Purpose Statement, you identified the major question that your book will ask and answer, and why your information is important to your readers.

Now, let's identify the vital components that will help you answer that overarching question and deliver on the promise made by your title and subtitle. These components provide the first layer of structure in your outline, and will show you exactly where to introduce each of your topics and talking points.

To begin, ask yourself the following Big Delivery Questions:

- *What specific information, habits, statistics, or life lessons will my readers need to learn* (about my subject/concept, themselves, or both) in order to create the result I've promised?

- *What foundational concepts do my readers need to understand* before they undertake a journey through my book? (Or, conversely, what core concepts can I assume that even novice readers will be familiar with?)

- *What action steps will my readers need to take* in order to create the result I've promised, and what information will they require before they are equipped to take those action steps?

To flesh out your answers, put each of the above questions at the top of a page (or on an index card, or on your whiteboard) and list as many responses as come to mind, without censoring or editing. Let your deeper knowledge of your topic come through.

Depending on your book concept, some of the answers will be obvious to you immediately. For example, if your book is titled *10 Steps to Greater Intimacy*, it is clear that your plan will include ten action steps, plus the information necessary to execute those action steps, an introductory discussion, and your conclusion statements. Once you know your ten action steps, you can identify how to equip readers to explore those steps in a way that creates the result you have promised.

Other times, the answers won't be so apparent, and you will have to dig deep into the heart of your concept to pull out your teaching points and action steps.

The establishment of your Information Delivery System is the most important part of your outlining process, so *don't skip it!* Take as much time as you need to feel completely clear about the journey your readers will undergo over the course of your book. If you feel burned out, take a break for a day. One day lost at this stage could save you weeks of rewrites later on!

Once you have exhausted your store of answers for each of your Big Delivery Questions, ask yourself:

- In what order will readers need to learn [the answers to Big Delivery Question 1] in order to create my intended result?
- In what order will readers want to implement [the action steps from Big Delivery Question 2] in order to create results, and feel comfortable and empowered in each action?

Now, take the information you've gathered, and arrange your content into learning steps that progress logically from introduction to end result. Think of it as creating a "curriculum" for your readers.

You may end up with dozens of steps, or just a few. The number of steps matters less than the clarity of each part of your process.

The most effective systems are those in which each step *builds on the step preceding it.* Whether your book is based on a timeline, a ladder or "step-by-step" system, a life story, or some other formula, it is best to start at the beginning and move in a straight line toward your conclusions, with each piece of the answer to your book's overall question presented in a logical order, and each new piece of information (or action step) building on the one before.

This logical progression of steps is your **Information Delivery System**—the formula you will follow through the rest of this chapter in order to lead readers through your book from start to finish.

If the process of arranging your Information Delivery System still feels challenging or unclear, here are some further hints:

- Begin with the basics, then move on to more complex or esoteric subjects once readers' understanding of your topic and viewpoint has been firmly established.

- When working in an "action step" system, start with the most basic step and proceed to the most complex. Alternately, structure the steps according to a timeline.

- When working with memoir, extensive stories, or case studies that progress over time, present your information in chronological order.

- When working within an existing system that is already broken up into parts—the seven chakras, the twelve major arcana, the four seasons, the twelve months—use the accepted order as the basis for your Information Delivery Systems's steps, with general or exploratory content preceding these items, and conclusions following.

Once you have completed these exercises, start to finish, you will start to see the basic shape of your book emerge from the fog, and understand exactly how you will deliver the promised results.

Pretty cool, huh?

Now, on a big piece of paper or a fresh word processor page, write down each step of your Information Delivery System in order, leaving plenty of space between each item. (Or, use your index cards, whiteboard, etc.)

Congratulations. You have just constructed the skeleton of your outline!

The next step is to brainstorm your topics and talking points.

OUTLINING STEP #2
BRAINSTORM YOUR TOPICS & TEACHING POINTS

"Brainstorming," as defined by its creator, Alex Faickney Osborn, is group process in which participants fire off as many ideas as possible in a limited time. It is designed to encourage lateral thinking, solve problems creatively, and spark new ideas. Participants are encouraged to think aloud, and share every idea they have, no matter how outlandish.

Over time, the definition of "brainstorming" has evolved to include an individual's process of unfiltered idea generation. To brainstorm alone, simply write down anything and everything that comes to mind about your topic. Again, this is a creative process, so it needs to take place in a non-judgmental way—meaning, don't try to assess your ideas or put them into context while you are still in idea-generation mode.

In this phase of outline creation, you will brainstorm all of the topics, stories, statistics, and information you want to include in your book.

In no particular order, list every topic you might possibly want to touch on in your book, every anecdote or interview you want to include, and every point you want to make—large and small, broad and narrow. Don't wonder where they will fit, or how you will angle them, just get them down on paper.

Once your own list is complete, you might choose to enlist help from friends, family, and colleagues, or even do an e-mail poll or a traditional group brainstorm. Ask, "If you were reading a book about [my topic], what messages or pieces of information would be important to you?" Add the results of your research to your existing list.

Brainstorming Hints

If you have never brainstormed before, or have had trouble remaining objective about your ideas during a brainstorm, you're not alone. The following are a few of my favorite techniques to help you get the most out of your brainstorming process.

- *Set a timer.* Write down every idea that comes into your mind for a set period of time (fifteen minutes is usually enough) and don't stop writing until the timer goes off. If there are still more ideas churning, set the timer for a further five or ten minutes—but again, don't stop writing until the timer goes off.

- *Write longhand.* Personally, I think longhand writing is best for this stage, because there is no chance that you will get distracted by e-mail, social media, or other attention-suckers during your brainstorm. There is also a ton of research that proves that, when you write longhand, you retain information better, are more focused, are less likely to censor yourself, and can tap more easily into your creative brain—all of which are conducive to this stage of your process.

- *Write in a dark room.* This is helpful if you tend to start analyzing your ideas the moment you write or type them. Take a pen and paper (not your computer) and sit in a dimly lit room. You should be able to see the shape of your hand against the paper, but not read the actual words you are writing. Then, set your timer, and brainstorm your list. You won't be able to read—or edit—what you have written until you turn the light on.

- *Meditate beforehand.* Taking time to quiet your mental chatter will almost certainly improve your creation sessions. Sit with your eyes closed, take a few deep breaths, and ask your creative self to step forward.

- *Ask your inner critic to back off.* Constant self-criticism is less-than-helpful during any part of the writing process—but now, when you are just allowing your ideas to blossom, it can be downright damaging. Before you brainstorm, ask your inner critic to step out for a while. Visualize him/her leaving the room—and then lock the door. Be gentle, but firm. This is *your* creative time.

OUTLINING STEP #3
SORTING YOUR TOPICS

Now that you have collected all of your topics, information, and notes in one place, it's time to start sorting.

Sorting your topics is like sorting laundry: everything is arranged according to specific criteria. In the case of your clothes, that might be lights, darks, whites, and delicates. In the case of your topics list, it will be broad topics, narrow topics, and tangents.

Your three topic types are:

- *Broad topics* are those which encompass a large amount of information, require a lot of exploration, or are central to the purpose of your book.
- *Narrow topics* are specific to one facet of an Information Delivery Step; they are the single "talking points" which require less information or explanation than your broad topics.
- *Tangents* are topics that relate only partially (or not at all) to the theme of your book and the steps in your Information Delivery System. You won't be working with these items until the rest of your outlining process is complete.

Create three separate lists, each on its own notebook page or in its own document file. One by one, assign your brainstormed topics to the most appropriate list.

If you're not sure where a particular topic belongs, add it to more than one list; you can play with placement later.

Pick Out Your Broad Topics

Your broad topics should naturally correlate to the central themes of your book, as well as to the steps of the Information Delivery System you generated in Step #1. (For example, in a book about natural healing, "nutrition" and "supplements" might be two of your broad topics.)

Your broadest topics—those which address an entire step or even two steps in your Information Delivery System—will become your chapters, while those that offer a substantial piece of a step will become subchapters. (Under your "nutrition" chapter topic, "good fats" might be a subchapter.)

Add your broad topics to your outline under the steps of your Information Delivery System. Don't worry about naming your chapters yet; just focus on getting your topics in order.

If you have broad topics that fall outside the scope of the structure you have created, ask yourself if they are actually a necessary piece of the answer to your book's overall question. If so, go back to Step #1 and work this topic into your information flow. If not, add it to your "tangents" list and move on.

Pick Out Your Narrow Topics

Once you have organized and assigned all of your broad topics, move on to your narrow topics.

Your *narrow topics* will form your subchapters, sections, and subsections. Most of them will fit naturally under one or more of your chapter topics. Some will even fit under other narrow topics. (To continue our example: Nutrition > Good Fats > Healthy Ways to Use Oil.)

If you think a narrow topic could work in more than one chapter, write it in both, and flag it for later analysis.

As with your broad topics, if any of your narrow topics don't fit easily into your Information Delivery Steps, put them on your "tangents" list.

OUTLINING STEP #4
CREATE CHAPTER TEMPLATES

By the time you have finished sorting, your outline will probably feel robust but disorganized—which is why your next step is to create a mini-Information Delivery System within each of your individual chapters so that your writing can flow naturally around and through your subtopics and information.

This flow is best accomplished by:

1. Ordering the chapter information in a linear way, and
2. Following a general chapter template

To begin creating flow in your chapters, ask yourself:

- *What specific question(s) does this chapter answer for readers,* and do my subchapters, sections, and subsections combine to answer this question? (If you haven't already, make note of the specific question for each chapter on your outline sheet. You will want to refer to this later.)
- *What do readers need to know about this chapter topic* before I present my main topic and subtopics?
- *How can I order my subchapters, sections, and subsections* so that each builds on the one before?
- *What information do my readers need to learn from this chapter* before they will be prepared to take the action steps I've identified and/or proceed to the next chapter/step?

This process is very like the one you used to create your Information Delivery System in Step #1. Work with the questions above until you feel comfortable with the flow of each chapter.

Once you have your information in order, you will want to apply a chapter template to your outline.

Chapter Templates

In general, you will follow the same formula, or template, for most of your chapters. (There are exceptions to this; I'll discuss them in a moment.)

Every inspirational or self-help book should follow some sort of structural guideline. Whatever the structure you choose to create for your chapters, your Information Delivery System should fit into it naturally.

Here is an overview of the three types of chapters, and where they belong in your book.

- *Your opening chapters* will explore the basic information readers need to know in order to get the most out of your book and fully understand the lessons you are imparting. You will explain your mission, your reasoning, and the how and why of your teaching angle. This is also your chance to share some of your personal story, introduce your tone and energy, and connect with readers in a big way. (You may also choose to place some of this information in your introduction, so you can jump right into your subject matter in Chapter 1.)

- *Your central chapters* will include your step-by-step exploration of your topic or action steps, according to your Information Delivery System.

- *Your final chapter* or chapters will sum up or restate your purpose, themes, and the most relevant information in your book; tie up loose ends; and reiterate your hopes for, and promises to, your readers.

In non-fiction writing, and especially in self-help and inspirational writing, it is important that each chapter unfolds in a consistent, predictable way. Like steadiness of tone, this repetition creates consistency and a sense of security for readers.

In practice, "consistency" in your chapters means that any stories or interviews, action steps, and other non-narrative components need to be positioned in *exactly* the same way in every chapter. Therefore, it is vital to apply a standard chapter template to all of your central chapters, and a variation of that same template to your opening and final chapters.

Sample Chapter Templates

{ Basic Chapter }

General information and definition of this chapter topic and why it is important to your readers

What readers will learn in this chapter

Subtopic 1

 Broad discussion of subtopic, including why it is important to readers

 Story/interview/research components and discussion of each

 Analysis of story/research/interview

 Conclusion statements

Subtopic 2

 Broad discussion of subtopic

 Story/interview/research components and discussion of each

 Analysis of story/research/interview

 Conclusion statements

Action steps and/or exercises for readers

Conclusion statements for chapter

{ General story-based chapter }

Adapt this model for books that rely heavily on memoir, interviews, or story components.

Primary story/interview/research component, which illustrates the general subject of this chapter and why it is important to readers

Discussion and teaching points related to main story component

New concepts, action steps, or inner truths revealed by story

Story/interview/research component 2

How this story relates to the primary story

Discussion of teaching points pulled from story

New concepts, action steps, or inner truths revealed by story

Conclusions

{ System-based book chapter }

Adapt this model for books based on existing systems (i.e., chakras, seasons, etc.)

Explanation/definition of this chapter topic and the specific component of the established system or series being applied.

How this component of established system or series relates to what you are teaching, and what knowledge it holds for readers

Story components, interviews, or examples, plus discussion of each

Subtopic 1

Relevant information, exercises, or action steps

Subtopic 2

Relevant information, exercises, or action steps

Ways to use this system component

Conclusion

{ Action-based book chapter, option #1 }

Adapt this model for books based on "steps" or a series of actions.

Explanation/definition of this chapter topic

Overview of chapter contents and what readers will learn

Action step

Describe action step and why it is important

Story/interview/research components and discussion of each

What this action step looks like in practice

Analysis of possible outcomes (including problems/questions readers might have)

Conclusion

{ Action-based chapter, option #2 }

Adapt this model for books based on "steps" or a series of actions which are complex, detailed, or multi-layered.

Overall goal of chapter, discussion of primary topic and action step(s), story element and related discussion

Tangible result of action steps

Action step 1

Details about how to accomplish this

Baby step 1
Baby step 2
Baby step 3

Possible pitfalls/questions

Action step 2

Details about how to accomplish this

Baby step 1
Baby step 2
Baby step 3

Possible pitfalls/questions

Chapter summary and conclusion

Adapt the above templates in any way you like, or create your own from scratch. (A fun exercise is to try to identify the chapter template for your favorite inspirational book.) You can try several different variations on your template, to see which one feels most natural to your Information Delivery System.

Include as many subchapters, sections, and subsections in each chapter as you want, as long as each of them contributes to the overall energy of the chapter (and the corresponding step in your Information Delivery System).

Keep in mind that your first chapter or two, as well as your conclusion chapter, might not follow your template exactly, and that's okay, because they have a purpose different to that of the rest of your book. Still, the closer you can keep to a single, consistent chapter format, the easier it will be for your readers to follow.

FINAL STEPS TO COMPLETE YOUR OUTLINE

By the time you have finished applying your Information Delivery System to your chapter template, you should have a more detailed picture of the structure of your book. Hooray!

Now, let's return to your one remaining list: your tangents.

Integrating Your Tangents

Your tangents are the topics that did not, at first glance, seem to fit in with any of your other broad or narrow topics, or in any step of your Information Delivery System.

Now that you have your chapter structures in place and filled out, some of these former "loners" might assign themselves naturally. Others, though, are still going to feel disconnected.

When considering where and how to place your tangent topics, ask yourself the following questions:

- *How important is this topic to my central purpose and theme?*
  - *It is very important*
    - Is there a way I could angle this topic to fit into one of my chapters?
    - Is it broad enough, and relevant enough to the rest of the material, to warrant its own chapter or step in my Information Delivery System?
  - *It is only moderately important:*
    - Why do I believe that this needs to be in my book?
    - Is there another topic already in my book which is closely related and to which I could assign this topic's story/info/statistics?
  - *I'm not sure if it is important*
    - Set it aside.
- *How important is this topic to my readers?*
  - *It is very relevant*
    - How can I restructure my chapter(s) to include this?
    - Do I plan to produce another book, article, or other piece of writing that could share this information with my readers?
  - *It is only moderately relevant*
    - Set it aside. Write an article or blog post on it at another time.
- *How relatable is this topic to my readers?*
- *How important is this topic to my conclusions?*

If, after you have asked these questions, you still can't decide whether to include your tangential topics or let them go, just set your list aside for later. Sometimes, potential locations for tangent topics won't reveal themselves until you actually start writing. However, doing this preliminary work with placement and context will reduce the likelihood that you will have to move or delete large sections of content around when it is time to work on your second draft.

Create Chapter and Subchapter Titles

Finally, the fun part you've been waiting for!

Now that you have all of your chapters, subchapters, and sections assigned under the umbrella of your Information Delivery System, it's time to name your chapters.

Chapter names should be short, succinct, and provide readers with a snapshot of what they can expect to learn in the chapter. They can also be fun, creative, and memorable—but above all, they should reflect the tone and character of your Purpose Statement, book title, subtitle, and overall message.

Here are some tips for creating great chapter titles:

- *Consider your book's title.* Chapter titles should align with your book title in format. If your book has a title like *5 Steps ...* you will need to use "Steps" in the title of each chapter that presents an action step.

- *Consider your tone.* A serious book with playful chapter titles will feel out-of-sync to readers. Same goes for a playful book with boring chapter titles. Again, look to your book's title for clues.

- *Be clear.* Remember, chapter titles are more than just headings; they are reference points. If they're vague or overly long, it may be harder for readers to find important information or re-read their favorite passages.

- *Be consistent.* Ideally, chapter titles should follow the same formula across the board. For example, if one of your chapter titles is a famous song lyric, all of your titles should be song lyrics. If you are using action verbs, the tense should be the same across the board. And if you are using simple descriptive word/noun combinations (i.e., Radical Thinking, Soothing Rituals) be sure that every chapter follows that same format and, if possible, uses the same number of words.

- *Use subtitles.* Consistency in chapter titling sometimes leaves less wiggle room to capture the essence of the chapter. Use subtitles to clarify the chapter's contents and focus your readers' energy.

At this point, you can probably see your book taking shape before your eyes. It's so exciting! Let that joy and exuberance fuel you as you move forward in your book creation process.

WHEN TO ADAPT YOUR OUTLINE AND/OR CHAPTER TEMPLATE

An outline is, in the end, a guide—a detailed, energetically sound guide, but a guide nonetheless. And sometimes, an alchemy occurs in the writing process that sends you off in a completely new and unexpected direction.

Maybe, while writing your first draft, you will come up with a slew of new ideas that didn't occur to you during your initial brainstorm. Maybe you will have so much to say on one chapter topic that it becomes a book unto itself. Maybe you will discover that your Information Delivery System doesn't work as smoothly as you thought it would. Maybe, in the process of writing and researching, you evolve one area of expertise to a new level, and implement a massive shift in your teaching platform. Or maybe there's another reason altogether.

You don't necessarily need to reconfigure your outline just because one (or more) of the above has happened. If you still feel that your book is aligned with your vision and purpose, there's no reason to make massive changes. (You might choose, for example, to take your new material and set it aside for Book Two.)

However, if your content has started to feel uncomfortable, irrelevant, dated, or misaligned, or if a slew of new questions have arisen around your material, you will want to revise (or totally recreate) your outline.

This happened to a client of mine. While working on a book which aimed to address all areas of life for women of a certain age, she realized that her true expertise lay in only one of these areas. Suddenly, a book about life turned into a book about starting a business. So, we created a new purpose statement and outline for the book, and her writing immediately started flowing again.

Don't beat yourself up over a shift like this. You haven't done anything wrong, and you haven't wasted your time! It's definitely better to shift course when the inspiration comes than run into the proverbial iceberg later. Plus, if your passion truly lies with your new material, that energy will absolutely translate to your book.

Any time you change your outline, take the time to go through the creation process again from start to finish, starting with a new Information Delivery System. Without that comprehensive overview of your book and its flow, you risk that your new content will stick out like a random refrigerator in the middle of a cornfield.

MOVING ON

Congratulations! You have created a detailed, comprehensive outline for your new inspirational book!

Now, the moment you've been waiting for … Drum roll please!

You're ready to write your *first draft*.

part 2

your creation process

chapter 3

YOUR DIVINE DOWNLOAD

(aka, Your First Draft)

U p until now, we have been working in an analytical space. We've outlined, structured, set parameters, and defined the path your book will take as you nourish it toward completion.

Now, it's time to *explore*.

POSITIVE VS. NEGATIVE STRUCTURE

Contrary to what you may have been told, creativity thrives within the bounds of structure. Having too many choices about what or how to write can be overwhelming, and can actually stifle creative thinking (or send you off on a wild goose chase).

The process you have just undertaken to determine your purpose, identify your tone, choose a title, set your intentions around your writing practice, and build your outline has created a strong foundation for your book, and (to follow through on the metaphor from Chapter 1) paved a clear path through the wild landscape of your creative mind.

Positive structure gives your writing direction. It harnesses the energy of your idea and points it at a target—which, of course, is the promise you have made to your readers, and the end result you want them to achieve. When your writing has direction, it is easier to stay focused, productive, and aligned with your purpose and vision.

However, it is important that your self-imposed boundaries don't become rigid or stressful. That energy creates a negative type of structure which feels restrictive and may actually deplete your creative energy.

To sum it up:

Positive Structure = Direction
Negative Structure = Restriction

What does this have to do with creating your first draft?

Just this: you are unique. Therefore, write in the way that feels best to you, and implement *only* the strategies that offer you positive structure.

Different people benefit from different amounts of planning. Personally, I like my bullet points and outlines, but when it comes to the details (like how to transition between subjects, or where to integrate anecdotes), I like to let things evolve organically. Sometimes this means I have to rewrite a section three or four times to get it perfect, but I don't mind, because I generate new ideas with each revision.

You, on the other hand, might be the kind of person who benefits from strategic planning in all phases of your creation process. Maybe your outline is twenty pages long, and you have mapped out every last shred of information. Great! As long as it keeps your energy focused and directed, run with it.

The real clue as to what is right for you is how you *feel* when it comes time to write. If you have a moderately detailed outline but still feel lost when you sit down to write, you might benefit from a greater amount of planning.

Planning, in the context of your first draft, might also mean choosing the ideal order in which to approach your chapters, sketching a secondary outline of the material you plan to work with in today's writing session, or gathering physical copies of your stories, statistics, and other materials before you sit down to work on a section.

Again, it's all about your personal preference. I prefer to tackle most books and e-books according to my outline, starting at Chapter 1—at least for my first draft. That way, I can easily build on what I've included in prior sections. If I receive a blockbuster idea that obviously belongs in a later chapter, I'll quickly sketch it out so I don't forget it, file it in the appropriate folder so I can find it later, and return to the topic at hand.

However, my approach reflects my preference for less planning and more spontaneity. If you have a really comprehensive outline, you might prefer a piecemeal approach, skipping from chapter to chapter and working on whatever you feel inspired to write that day. When everything is fully mapped out for you, there's less chance you will forget important story elements or information when skipping around.

Are you ready to get started?

THE MOST IMPORTANT STEP TO WRITING YOUR FIRST DRAFT

Write. Just write.

Write without censoring or editing your words.

Write without wondering how it will all come together.

Put words on the page, and keep putting words on the page until you have no more to say on your subject.

That's it. Start writing, and show up for your writing practice until your first draft is done.

There is no magic bullet when it comes to writing your first draft. There are no shortcuts. You must put the flesh of words around the skeletons of your ideas, and expand your concepts until they feel *alive* to your readers. Only when your ideas embody this aliveness can they be fully understood, implemented, and acted upon.

Some days, this will be laughably easy. Some days, it will make you want to scream. As with any practice that creates transformation, it's all part of the process.

What a First Draft Really Looks Like

If I can make one request of you, writer, it's that you remember this vital truth: no one, and I mean *no one*, is capable of writing a perfect first draft. Even the greatest writers need several rounds of revisions (and the input of a good editor) before their works are ready for public consumption.

Revisions aren't only necessary if your writing is poor. They are an integral part of the writing process. No matter how "good" your first draft is, you will still need to complete a second draft, and a third, and maybe even a fourth.

Before you get discouraged, allow me to present an analogy.

Think about your book as a beautiful wood carving. First, you do the hard work to coax the basic shape out of a block of wood. Then, you refine that shape until it is recognizable. After that, you refine it again, until it is beautiful and balanced. Finally, you sand it with progressively finer grades of sandpaper to get rid of splinters and bring out the wood's natural beauty. All of these steps must be completed before the work is ready to be seen and appreciated.

Every carving, no matter how large or small, goes through this gradual unveiling. Your writing process is exactly the same. The most you can expect from your first draft is to be able to see the basic shape of your book emerging from the piles of words on your pages.

Perfectionist tendencies and self-criticism can be truly counterproductive at this tender stage of your book's gestation—because, again, *your first draft will be a mess.* However, just as you wouldn't sand and polish your rough-hewn carving (because that would be silly) you should resist the urge to edit your first draft.

The best thing you can do right now is give yourself permission to color outside the lines, and make a mess all over your pages. You will have plenty of time (and lots of support from me) to clean things up in your second draft.

OUT OF YOUR HEAD AND ONTO THE PAGE

The most powerful thing you can do—now, and at every stage of your writing practice—is to simply show up, be present, and write.

However, as I (and every writer I've ever met) can personally attest, this is easier said than done.

Here are some tips to help you get the guts of your book out of your head and onto the page.

Free Writing vs. Directed Writing

There are two kinds of writing you can employ when creating your first draft: free writing and directed writing.

Free writing is just that: free.

To free write, simply pick a topic and run with it. Don't form paragraphs, or even sentences. Don't try to organize. Just write with the same honesty, introspective clarity, and immediacy that you usually bring to your journaling practice.

Free writing helps you get to the heart of the matter, and exposes your deepest thoughts and feelings. It also opens an unobstructed channel to your higher mind/divine self, and invites deeper wisdom and knowing to come through. This form of writing is perfect for helping you flesh out your more esoteric concepts and uncover what you really know and feel about a subject.

Directed writing is more structured. This is the kind of writing we use most often when writing with an end product in mind (as opposed to journaling, which is writing for the sake of the process). This kind of writing serves best when you are making an argument; referencing studies, facts, or figures; and creating action steps or exercises. It takes your energy and channels it into a fixed, narrow structure in order to create a particular outcome.

Most writers can, and should, use a combination of both kinds of writing when working on a first draft. Free writing might serve you best when starting a new chapter or subchapter, so that you can fully align with the deeper concepts and energies of the new material. Directed writing can then fill in the sections of your chapter templates using the products of your free writing as a basis.

Turn Off Your Inner Censor

Every time you hit the backspace or delete button, you press pause on your creative flow.

At this stage, let go of every form of editing and censorship you usually impose in your writing. Don't fix spelling errors. Stop checking your punctuation. Don't format your paragraphs. Basically, avoid anything that forces you to stop writing, correct, and restart.

If you have trouble doing this on your laptop, you could try writing longhand (maybe even in a dark room, like you did when you brainstormed your outline). Then, type up each section after you have finished writing.

Free Yourself From Interruption

Uninterrupted time is key to keeping your creative juices flowing. When it's time to start your writing practice, turn off your cell phone, log out of your e-mail, close your browsers, and commit to doing only one thing for the duration of your practice time. If you need to stop writing to access a piece of research or retrieve notes from a different file, be sure you don't get distracted on your way back to your page.

If children, family members, or roommates share your space, communicate your need to step away for the duration of your practice. Let them know that they should only interrupt you if the house is burning down, or if some other real catastrophe occurs. If you have little ones, ask a family member or sitter to come over while you write, or write during nap time.

At the time of this book's release, my daughter Áine is twenty-two months old. If I try to write with no support while she's awake, it's always a disaster. I end up feeling guilty on two fronts: not being present for her, and not being present for my writing. Thankfully, my awesome husband and some generous family members usually ensure that everyone gets what they need during my writing time.

Give Yourself What You Need to Stay Focused

Believe it or not, writing alone in a silent room is not always the best way to connect to your practice. In fact, for some of us, too much silence can feel downright stifling.

Here are some things that I, and the writers I interviewed for this book, do to get and stay focused.

- *Write in public.* Getting out of the house also gets you out of your to-do list. Plus, for some, the buzz of conversation in a busy place acts like white noise, and actually aids focus.

- *Write in nature.* Natural surroundings stimulate creative energy. Taking your book to a park or just to your back deck can add some new juice and joy to your writing practice.

- *Change your viewpoint.* Turn your desk toward, or away from, your window. Move your laptop to the dining room table, or the couch, or the front porch. Even a small change can shift your perspective.

- *Put on some music.* YouTube has whole channels dedicated to "study music." If you're not a fan of Mozart or trance/yoga music, put on anything you like—but if you tend to be easily distracted by lyrics, instrumental is the way to go. You could also play music in a foreign language.

- **Wear headphones.** Regular or noise-cancelling headphones are a great way to tune out noises and distractions.

- *Take a "reconnection break."* If you really can't concentrate, take a break. Take a walk outside, or indulge in a long shower. Think about what you really want to say, and let those ideas sink into your body. Then, when you feel refreshed, come back to your desk and start over.

- *Meditate.* Connecting to your book on an energetic level is a great way to align your energy with your intention, and get back on track.

A Sample Meditation for Book Writing

Sit quietly with your spine straight and your hands cupped in your lap.

Visualize orange and golden light energy flowing down on you from above. This is the light of your divine source and your higher self. Feel it flow through every part of your body—into your arms, hands, torso, legs, and feet. This light illuminates you from the inside, and elevates the vibration of every cell.

Then, see that light energy flowing out of your hands and collecting in your cupped palms. Imagine your book taking shape in your hands, emerging from the light as a direct result of your creative energy and focus.

When you can fully feel your book in your hands, thank your higher self (and any higher beings who assisted you), and know that you have already created your book's energetic imprint in this reality.

Open your eyes, take a deep breath, and dive in to today's writing practice!

Warm Up Your "Writing Muscles"

Sometimes, writing is like dancing: we need to get warmed up before the magic can happen. And sometimes, our brains don't want to do the same thing for our warmup as we're doing for our performance.

If you're not feeling particularly connected to one of your subjects on a given day, here are some things you can do to warm up and flex your writing muscles.

Work with a journaling prompt question. Choose one from an online source, or create your own by asking a question or creating an imaginary scenario. Write longhand for a page or two to get focused, then transition to working on your book.

Quiz yourself. Instead of trying to write cohesive paragraphs, do a brain dump on the subject you are working with today. Set a timer for five minutes, and write at the top of the page, "*What I know about* ____." List as many facts, ideas, opinions, and stories as you can about your subject before the timer goes off. Don't stop to format, punctuate, or organize. You may be shocked at how much information is actually in your head about your subject! Once you finish your brain dump, pick the bits which most closely correspond with the section of your outline you are following, and write in-depth about those.

Create a "Crystal Clause."
This jump-starts your creativity by asking you to look at the same phrase (aka, clause) in many different ways. It is also great practice for writing in general. Here's how to do it: Write a short phrase or sentence about your topic. Then, write a series of at least five related phrases which say the same thing (or close to the same thing) in different ways.

You can work with parallel statements, opposite statements, and even tangents. These are the "facets" of your crystal, and they are amazing for helping you make your point in a definitive way without saying the same thing over and over.

Here's an example of a Crystal Clause:

- *Main Phrase*: Love is the answer to everything.
- *Crystal Clause 1:* When you have a question, you can always answer it with love.
- *Crystal Clause 2:* No problem exists that cannot be solved with love.
- *Crystal Clause 3:* When you don't know the answer, ask yourself, "What is the most loving way to proceed?"
- *Crystal Clause 4:* Hatred is not a solution.

The Crystal Clause not only helps you warm up your brain, but can also force you think critically about your topic and the way you approach it.

Jump to another section in your outline, and work there instead. (As I mentioned earlier, this is easiest if you have a comprehensive, detailed outline.) If you feel strongly about the process of writing your book "in order," simply do a brain-dump session as described above on a subject further along in your book. This is helpful in two ways: first, it helps you empty your head of extra information; and second, it generates notes for you to reference later.

PLANNING FOR "STUCK PLACES" (AKA, WRITER'S BLOCK)

No matter how great your outline, or how innate your knowledge of your topic, there are going to be places in your book that make you feel stuck in the mud. Your metaphorical feet, which had been running (or at least walking steadily) up to this point, will suddenly refuse to move, and you will feel like you can't make an inch of real progress.

Just as there are some areas of your life which flow easily, and others which require more attention and deliberation, so too will there be sections of the path through your first draft which are more challenging and take more time.

This is natural, and it happens to everyone at one point or another. (It happened to me: Chapter 2 of this book was a doozy! I had to revise it five times.) Therefore, it is helpful to create a plan for navigating these blockages so they don't paralyze you.

If you find yourself stuck on a certain chapter, section, or concept, here are some ways to get back in the flow.

> *Ask your inner circle for support.* If you have willing friends, a good editor, or other people you can rely on for assistance, ask them to brainstorm with you, or even play "devil's advocate." Talking out your subject often provides the perspective you need to jump-start your creative thinking.

> *Join a writers' group—but make sure it's a good fit.* The energy of the group is more important than the focus. It would be better to join a fiction writers' group where you feel supported by the collective (and where you can hone your storytelling skills) than a group in your genre where everyone snipes at one other!

Ask for higher guidance. Connect with your higher power, higher self, or whatever energy assists you in your creative process. Ask to be shown what you need to learn, do, or receive in order to be able to communicate this concept in an effective way.

Journal about it. Write out these questions, then allow the answers to emerge.

- What about this concept/chapter/section is challenging for me?
- What am I not allowing myself to know, see, or feel about this subject?
- What questions do I need to ask right now?
- What support do I need to receive in order to write about this subject with ease, grace, and confidence?

LIVING YOUR LESSONS

Most of the time, we get stuck because we are in a learning curve of some sort. If you go through the above exercises and ask all of your questions, and still find yourself mired and struggling to write, you might be "living your lessons."

Especially for those of us who specialize in transformation, personal growth, spiritual practices, and healing, the writing process can—and probably will—trigger multiple parts of our personal unfinished business. As they say, "You teach what you need to learn." A book, by its nature, includes a lot of material, and the scope of that material is far deeper and broader than that required by other mediums (like blog articles or workshop sessions). Somewhere along the way, you might come across a piece of your own knowledge that you have been avoiding, or that you haven't mastered fully in your own life.

Don't judge yourself for this; you haven't failed in any way! You haven't suddenly become a non-expert on your subject, or lost the right to teach others, or disappointed your readers. There may simply be some crucial energy or understanding that won't become available to you until you complete another piece of your book. Or, you may be about to experience some vital life lesson that will take this "stuck place" to a whole new level.

You can't know the cause right now, so don't judge the outcome.

You will know you are living your lessons when things start to get *heavy*. You will struggle with your ideas, question your motives, and doubt yourself for no good reason. You will get full-on writer's block. The stuff you are writing about will start cropping up all over your life, and attempt to distract you from your creation process.

But through all of this, no matter how hard the proverbial shit hits the fan, I implore you:

KEEP WRITING

Even if your writing process feels more like journaling than like writing a book, keep writing.

Write longhand, if your computer is too distracting.

Write at 3 a.m., when your nervous mind wakes you up.

Write when you are weeping, or raging, or trembling in fear.

The immediacy of your experience during these challenging times, and the raw emotion underpinning those experiences, will soon become a powerful point of connection for your readers.

You may not end up using all of what you produce during this time—but I promise you that, if you keep writing, you will work through it faster, and learn more from it, than if you run away from it. Avoidance is a coping mechanism, not a long-term strategy.

As you work through your personal growth curve (and continuously write and journal about your process) you can also work on other sections of your book. This is a great way to give your mind and spirit a break from the drama while still moving toward your greater goal.

If you are stuck on the section about relationships, write the section about business. If you are stuck on money, write about love. If there is nothing at all in your book that doesn't touch on the lesson you are living, create some exercises to help yourself (and soon, your readers) through this tough spot.

But whatever you do, *keep writing!*

THE CREATIVE FLOW:
YOUR FIRST DRAFT AND YOUR OUTLINE

If you are struggling with your writing, but can't clearly identify the issue as living your lessons or garden variety writer's block, there is another possibility to be considered.

Remember when I said, back in Chapter 2, that your outline is fluid? That it may change as you write your book? Your first draft is the first place where you may discover a need to adjust your outline.

"So," you ask, "How can I tell when it's time to make a change?"

The best way to identify when to shift your outline is a feeling of being trapped or bound by your outline. Remember, positive structure = direction, negative structure = restriction. If you feel that your outline won't allow you to say what you need to say on your subject, or doesn't give a particular concept enough room to unfold completely, it may be time to reassess. You may also discover that one chapter can become a book unto itself, or that one section needs to become a chapter.

Before you charge ahead, though, let me share this: a need for expansion is the *least common reason* why writers change their outlines. Much more common is the desire to avoid those stuck places we talked about earlier. In order to avoid living their lessons, or diving into their own vulnerability, writers will literally expunge challenging topics from their outlines. However, this avoidance serves neither the book nor the writer, and almost always leaves the book feeling just that little bit "unfinished."

In order to avoid shortchanging your book (and your own growth process), or trapping yourself in a constant cycle of outline revision, you will want to meditate on and journal about your feelings and reasoning before you start dismantling your structure.

Ask yourself:

- What are the truest reasons I want to change my outline? (*Note: You may need to write out all of your "surface," cognitive reasons before you get through to your emotional reasons.*)
- Is my desire to change based in fear? Is there something in my original structure that I'm avoiding—something that would require me to expose my emotions, opinions, fears, or vulnerability?
- If my desire is fear-based, am I ready and willing to face this fear in order to move forward?
- Is my change based on an avoidance (fear-based or otherwise) of my stuck places? If so, can I work through these challenges to honor the structure I've created?
- Does this decision to change the outline feel expansive or restrictive to me?

The truest way to identify expansion vs. restriction is to feel it in your body. When you ask yourself questions about your outline and your reasons for changing it, does your body tighten up? Does your energy move downward, forming a tight knot in your belly, bowels, or heart? Or does it move upward, and expand outward through your throat, third eye, or the crown of your head?

Asking simple yes-or-no questions, and paying attention to your body's energetic responses, is a great way to tap into your inner wisdom and move through challenges in any part of your writing process.

What To Do When Your Book Changes Direction

It happens sometimes. You feel light and expansive about making a change to your outline, and you *know* you are doing it for the right reasons.

Great! Now where do you go from here?

If your whole book suddenly takes a hard left turn, the best thing to do is start back at the very beginning. Write a new Purpose Statement. Create new title ideas. Play with the energy of this new book and make sure it fits you like a glove.

Then, redo your entire outline.

Yes, your *entire outline*. Start to finish. No cutting and pasting.

Create a brand new Information Delivery System. Then, brainstorm and assign your chapter topics, and refine your chapter templates, just like you did the first time. This process will help you get fully connected to the new direction you are taking, and ensure that your new topic is deep and broad enough to fill a book.

WHEN YOUR FIRST DRAFT IS COMPLETE

How do you know when your first draft is done?

You'll know. You'll sense it—a shift in the energy of your book, a sense of wholeness and cohesiveness that wasn't there before.

But just in case you aren't sure, here is the measurement:

Your first draft is complete when you have written at least the raw basics of each chapter, subchapter, and section created in your outline. Once you have that foundation, you will be ready to move on to your second draft.

But first, let's explore one of the most important components of any inspirational book:

Story.

chapter 4

THE HUMAN CONNECTION

Story As a Teaching Tool

S tories weave the fabric of our lives. They are our memories, our perceptions, our very identities. The stories we tell ourselves and others speak volumes about the way we see the world, and our own place within it.

As humans, we learn through sharing stories. When we listen to others speak about their experiences, actions, reactions, and emotions, we integrate their experiences into our own. (And thank goodness for that! Otherwise we would all need to jump off a ledge to learn about gravity, or put our hands on hot stoves to know that fire will burn us!)

When we want to share how we feel with others, we tell stories. When we want others to understand our experiences, we tell stories. When we want to communicate an esoteric or lofty idea, we create a fable or a metaphor. Even our dearly-held opinions are stories about our beliefs.

Understanding the ways in which stories are woven into our identities is vital to your writing. Your own stories, and the ways in which you tell them, will enable you to harness this powerful tool of human connection and bring it to bear on your chosen subject.

WHAT ARE YOUR STORIES?

If someone asked you to tell the story that defines your life, what would that story be?

This story reveals volumes about who you are. It also determines the types of people who will be attracted to you (and by extension, to your book). Therefore, if you choose to use your own story as a component of your book, be sure it is both powerful and authentic.

Anthropologist Robin Ridington once wrote, "Stories are a spirit net." That net captures those who are of like mind and energy, and draws them into your innermost world.

Linda Joy, founder of Inspired Living Publishing, used this fundamental truth as the basis for her signature Authentic Storytelling Model™. She encourages her authors to dig deep and uncover their truest emotions, beliefs, and motivations to create stories that speak to women around the world and attract their ideal clients.

I've worked with Linda since 2010 to hone and streamline this storytelling format, and in those years I've seen firsthand what well-told stories reveal about their authors. Moreover, I've learned that authentic stories are the most powerful leverage you have with readers, no matter what your subject or genre, because nothing connects people on an emotional level more completely than a good story.

WHEN TO USE STORY

If you are reading this chapter for the first time, you are probably working on your first draft, and may be struggling with where to include story in your book.

Chances are, there are a few stories you knew you would need to tell when you conceptualized this book—for example, the story of how you came to learn and teach this material. However, there are probably several other places in your narrative that could benefit from story. In fact, in most cases, I'd suggest including at least one story (or case study, if that is your format) in every chapter of your book.

There are some things that story can do more effectively than any other type of narrative. For example, a good story can help readers:

- Relate on a deep, emotional level to you and your topic.
- See themselves as candidates for your help and advice.
- Understand that they are not alone.
- Visualize how your processes and techniques can be applied in real life and what tangible results they can create.

You can also use story to:

- Introduce a new concept or talking point.
- Illustrate a major revelation in your narrative.
- Show how taking certain steps created real change in someone's life.
- Give readers an understanding of who you were and what you experienced during different points in your own growth process.
- Allow readers to see exactly how you arrived at the conclusions and knowledge you share in the book, and why you are passionate about this material.
- Provide a break from "teaching voice," which engages readers in a different way. (More on Teaching Voice later in this chapter.)

As you read through the rest of this chapter and learn about the vast potential of story as a teaching tool, you will probably see many more places in your outline where you can use story to enhance and expand on your topics, and better answer your book's core questions.

WHAT MAKES STORIES POWERFUL

The contents and perspectives of our personal stories define us, but they aren't necessarily what others connect to. What connects people through the network of story is *emotion*.

Have you ever felt that you could truly put yourself in a character's shoes, even if the events of the story were so dramatic or fantastical that you could never imagine them happening in real life? This connection isn't based on what happens in the story, but rather on your ability to relate to the *emotions* the character experiences as events unfold.

A great example of this effect can be found in Disney's blockbuster movie, *Frozen*—a movie my toddler begs to watch every single day.

This movie didn't become a worldwide phenomenon because Elsa could shoot ice out of her hands, or because Kristoff had a talking reindeer friend. No one in the world (that I know of) can relate to either of those things. No, the reason this movie was, and is, so popular is that nearly every person who watches it can relate on a soul-deep level to Elsa's fear and shame, and to Anna's steadfast belief in someone she loves, even though that person doesn't love herself. Those story components, along with a few other central themes (like the snowman with an impossible dream), make this movie accessible to nearly anyone in the world, regardless of age, gender, religion, or experience.

To sum it up: *emotion begets connection*.

Many writers fall into the trap of thinking that the "what" and "why" of their stories are more important than the emotional components. They believe that if they *tell* readers what happened (and how, and why), it will create a bridge. In some cases, that may be true—but most of the time, this approach will actually create a barrier.

Relying on story events alone to create a relationship with your readers is like opening a restaurant that only serves spaghetti. Yes, some people will *totally* understand that spaghetti is the best food in the world—but others who share your love of Italian cooking might prefer *penne alla vodka*, and if you don't find a way to bridge that gap, they'll go elsewhere for their meal.

Okay, maybe that example is a bit trite. So let's try it this way.

Let's say you were attacked by a stranger on the street, and your healing story is a foundational piece of your book. The how and why of your attack may (unfortunately) be relatable to some of your readers.

But here's the thing: even those readers who had similar experiences to yours will not be relating to the events you describe, because they didn't live your event; they lived their own. Instead, they will be relating to the *emotions* which arise within them when they remember their own trauma. Then, they will transpose their emotion onto your story, and *imagine* that you felt the same way they did.

This phenomenon of "transference of emotion" creates empathy and connection, and is one of the reasons why survivor's groups and support groups work so well. But unless you add strong emotional components to your writing which allow those readers who haven't shared your experience to *feel what you were feeling* at the moments when the events of your story were taking place, this transference will not work at all. Although your "non-experienced" readers can theorize about how you must have felt in those moments, it is a cognitive understanding only; they can't really *imagine* it, and they can't feel it in their bodies.

In fact, bald statements of events with no emotion or feeling attached may actually push non-experienced readers away, because they might think your book is not really meant for them.

In order to include *all* of your readers, regardless of their experiences, and make your concepts accessible to people of all backgrounds, write your stories with a focus on emotion.

This doesn't mean you shouldn't share events and action in your story. It only means that events should be treated as the triggers for your emotional experiences, not as the sole focus of the narrative.

Show vs. Tell: What Emotional Writing Looks Like

If you have done any formal study of writing at all, you have probably heard the axiom, "Show, don't tell."

This must be great advice, since nearly every writing teacher gives it—but what does "showing" look like in practice?

"Showing" readers what happened through story takes them a step beyond emotional connection into a real-time experience. To illustrate this discussion, I have created a series of examples based on my personal story.

Example #1: Telling

Here is a little snippet of my personal story.

> After living with my alcoholic husband for nearly eight years, I finally moved out.

Let's be honest. I'll bet you read that and thought, "So what?"

In that snippet of story, there is no emotion. There is also no sense of process—of movement from one emotional place to another; it's simply a statement of fact. This is what we think of as "telling" the story.

Example #2: Emoting

Here's the same story with a focus on emotion.

> Why did I stay in a marriage with an alcoholic for eight years? I suppose I was afraid that there was nothing better out there for me. The day I finally moved out, I was shaking so hard I could barely lift my suitcase—but I'd reached an internal breaking point. Being all alone in the world was no longer as frightening as living with a ticking time bomb.

Not too many more words, but a whole lot more substance. You probably tapped into a little bit of what I was feeling in that moment; after all, not everyone has been in an abusive relationship, but everyone has been scared of change.

However, in this "emotive" writing, I haven't given you a single extra detail about actual events, and there is no action to drive the narrative forward.

Example #3: Showing

Now, I'll *show* you the moment when I left my first marriage.

The phone woke me up.

"I just got to work. Are you ..." An awkward pause. "Are you still leaving?"

Outside my window, the leaves were just starting to turn, and the sunlit yard looked hazy and surreal. It was warm for September, but I was shivering. Today was the day. There was no going back. I'd made a promise to him, and to myself.

"Yes," I whispered. "I'll be gone before you get home."

As soon as I hung up, I jumped out of bed. I'd told him the night before what I intended to do, but I was terrified that he'd renege on his agreement to let me go without a fight. Any second, he could decide to leave work, come home, and try to stop me—and if he did, would there be a half-liter of whiskey between work and where I was? Would it be my sad-eyed, gentle husband who showed up, or the snarling monster who lived in the bottle?

There was no way to know—and no time to waste.

I tossed clothes into suitcases without folding them. My shoes went into paper bags. I stuffed my laptop into its case, and my books into boxes. I took the good pots and pans (he didn't cook, so he wouldn't miss them) but left all the dishes. He'd smashed half of the plates last week, anyway.

Into the car went the rest of the worldly possessions I couldn't live without: the yoga figures my sister had painted for me; my guitar, keyboard, and microphone.

I started to grab the violin he'd given me—the one that had belonged to his dead brother—but just as quickly put it back in the corner. It wasn't worth the fight.

When my car was full, I took one last look around the apartment that had been my home for so long. It looked foreign, strange, as if I'd blundered into the wrong house by accident. I wasn't sad. I didn't feel anything really, except a strange, buzzing excitement. My soul had been screaming for change for years. Now, I had my parachute on, and I was ready to leap. He hadn't shown up to stop me. Just a few more steps, a few more breaths, and I would be free.

"Showing" is a combination of action and emotion. The actions aren't the big "overview actions" or statements of fact I demonstrated in Example #1, but rather the immediate actions taken by the central character (in this case, me) which move the story along and provide clues as to the character's emotional state.

For example, even if I hadn't told you I was panicked, you would have inferred it by the way I packed my suitcases. This action matches the energy of what I told you in the previous paragraphs. However, if I told you I was panicked, but then proceeded to methodically fold my clothes into the suitcases, and box up all of my books in alphabetical order, that wouldn't make much sense (unless you already knew from previous parts of the story that I was meticulously neat, and that chaos made my anxiety worse).

My choice to leave the violin tells you that I was afraid of giving my ex reasons to contact me. The observation about the dishes tells you that violent outbursts were common in our home. The relief and elation I experienced after the packing was done tells you that my emotional state had shifted as a result of my actions.

Without going into backstory, and in the space of a single page, my "showing" exercise has given you a snapshot of my first marriage and the reasons I made such a drastic change.

Now, if I was writing a book about taking charge of your life, I might follow this story with a discussion about how working through fear can be empowering, or how we often let our fear of others' reactions determine our choices. You, the reader, are now (hopefully) feeling some of the same emotions I was feeling on the day in question, because you were able to connect with the targeted actions and emotional elements of my story. So, when I open my discussion on working through fear, you will have an emotional stake in the "outcome"—i.e., the lesson I'm aiming to teach you.

How much showing is too much?

Let's face it: humans are complicated creatures. Especially in times of great stress or transition, we can feel multiple emotions at once, many of which are contradictory to one another!

For example, on a normal day I'd say it was impossible to feel scared, happy, sad, angry, confused, optimistic, and defeated all at the same time. Yet I felt all of those things on the day I left my first marriage. My emotions overlapped each other like waves, tossing me in a million different directions.

However, if I had tried to explain all of these feelings to you in the context of my story, or use actions to illustrate them all, I would have led you hopelessly off-track, and probably mired the narrative in backstory. In order to keep the story moving, I chose the two most powerful emotions—fear and excitement—and worked with those.

When "showing" readers a concept through story (whether your own story or someone else's) it is helpful to focus on one or two central emotions and the actions which illustrate those emotions. These emotions should be not only relatable to your readers, but also central to the teaching point of the section or chapter your story is supporting.

This can be challenging, especially when you are working with your own story, because you know that there were other things that happened besides what you are sharing. However, leaving out contradictory elements or extraneous details isn't cheating your readers; nor will it make your story less authentic. In fact, by focusing only on the vital details and actions, you are streamlining the path to understanding for your readers and allowing them to experience the exact emotional state you will be exploring (or attempting to shift) in the next part of your discussion.

With practice, you will be able to implant and showcase major themes and topics in your stories by using words and actions to call attention to specific focal points. Remember: the more words you spend on an action, feeling, or event, the more important it will seem to your readers.

When you create "showing" stories, think about them as scenes in a movie. What would viewers see? What would they not see? Try to keep most of the action in real time, instead of constantly flashing back or "telling" about events that happened previously.

When possible, use action to convey the central character's feelings. For example, instead of *telling* readers, "I was incredibly nervous," *show* yourself pacing the carpet or fiddling with the loose threads on your shirt (or whatever you do when you're nervous). Most of the time, readers will be able to infer emotion through your actions—and it will be a more powerful inference because they will not only be empathizing with you, but vicariously living your actions alongside you.

Telling, Emoting, and Showing:
When to use each of the three storytelling modes

There is a time and place for each of the three storytelling modes I described in the previous section. Although "showing" is always the preferred method when creating teaching stories, the other two forms can also be useful if applied strategically.

The following is a summary of when and how to use each storytelling format.

Example #1: Telling or "story overview"
Use this mode when:

- You are reviewing events shown in a previous story.

- The facts of certain events are necessary to readers' understanding of an upcoming story, but are not emotionally significant to readers or relevant to your teaching point.

Example #2: Emoting
Use this mode when:

- You are recalling or reiterating emotions for readers in order to drive home a teaching point.

- You want to show an internal emotional shift which did not depend on outward actions or experiences (this usually happens as an interjection in the greater story narrative).

- The events of the accompanying story are insignificant in the greater context of the narrative. (For example if you experienced an internal shift while lying in bed, you don't need to spend two paragraphs describing what's happening in the room).

Example #3: Showing
Use this mode when:

- You want readers to deeply connect to the story in order to absorb the lessons you are imparting.

- You want to show how shifts in emotion or understanding paralleled shifts in the main character's physical situation.

- You want to utilize dramatic elements.

OH, THE *DRAMA!*

When you use "showing" stories as teaching elements, you will begin to notice something. The best stories, the ones that make the most profound impact, are full of *drama*.

> **Drama:** \\'drä-mə\\: *a state, situation, or series of events involving an interesting or intense conflict of forces.**

Drama is the result of conflict, and conflict is the result of our human reactions to events. In other words, events don't create drama, people do.

Whenever we attack, avoid, blame, shame, deny, ignore, or in some other way refuse to accept and flow with an event or situation, there is drama. When we come to an understanding, accept the change, and take the necessary actions to move forward, the drama is resolved. The events might be finished, or they might still be happening, but it doesn't matter because we are no longer in conflict with them.

This process of identification, conflict, and resolution is the basis of nearly every story ever told, fictional or otherwise. When we can observe someone's process through conflict and into growth, we develop an identification with that person. Great characters stick in our heads, because we have intimately followed them from drama into resolution.

In an inspirational book, the importance of your readers' identification with your stories goes beyond mere character development or memorability. It literally becomes the vehicle by which you will effect change, and eventually resolution, in some aspect of your readers' own real-life drama.

In order to create this "crossover" effect in its fullness, your readers must identify on a deep level with the conflict in your stories. In other words, they need to feel the emotions of your story subjects as fully and intimately as possible, so that they can also experience what it will feel like once that conflict is resolved.

This means that you will need to dig deep when writing your stories. If you are using the stories of others, your interviews will need to include compelling emotional descriptions and components. If you're using your own story, you will need to put yourself back in the mental and emotional space you occupied before your conflict was resolved, and channel the emotions you felt at that time as fully as possible.

This is where, in my opinion, many writers fall short.

I know, I know. You *hate* drama. You have only just weeded it out of your life, and you don't want to go back there ever again. But in inspirational writing, drama is an integral part of teaching—so you will need to get over your aversion to drama (an aversion which, ironically, can create a *ton* of drama in your writing process) and instead embrace drama's enormous value and potential.

Why is drama vital to inspirational writing?

Have you ever had a friend who just seems to have it all together? When you ask about her life, she tells you how great it is, and how everything is working perfectly. You're happy for her, but when you look at those same areas in your own life, you see a big old mess. You don't quite understand why she has it all together, and you don't. (There might even be a sneaky undercurrent of jealousy there.)

The thing is, when your friend talks about how great things are, you aren't seeing her *process*, only the result. You don't see how she struggled to do those morning meditations, or how she had to weed seventeen extraneous commitments out of her life to have the time to launch her super-successful blog. Maybe she told you about these challenges while they were happening, but you don't remember them now. All you can feel, at this moment, is that you want some of what she has.

As the author of an inspirational book, *you* are that enviable friend to your readers. The past is past, the drama is behind you, and you are excited to show everyone what life looks like on the other side.

Great! That's why we write inspirational books.

However, readers who are still on the "dark side" of their own dramas *will not relate at all* to where you are right now, just as you sometimes have trouble relating to your friend. To bridge this gap, your readers will need to be *shown* the uncomfortable place where you started, and guided along the path you forged, with you (and your other story subjects) walking beside them the whole way. Otherwise, they'll look at you standing tall atop your mountain, and say, "There is no way I can get there. I just can't see the path."

The drama in your stories can be internal or external. It can be physical, mental, emotional, or spiritual. But in order for your teaching stories to be effective, it *needs* to be there. So when you tell your teaching stories, start at the beginning, craft the narrative through "showing," and include actions that readers can experience alongside you (or your subjects). Then, lead them honestly and authentically through the drama to the conclusion—which, ultimately, is all or part of the promise made by your book.

If you can do that, you will have loyal readers for life.

CRAFTING DIALOGUE

Dialogue is a powerful component of storytelling. Entire books have been written on how to use dialogue to its greatest effect; if your book relies heavily on story elements, it may be worth your time to read a few. (I've listed a few of my favorites in the resources section.)

The format of this book doesn't allow me to explore the subtle mechanics of dialogue at length, but I do want to share a few tips for making your story conversations pop.

When to Use Dialogue

If, in your story, you find yourself writing something like ...

> While we were standing in the kitchen, he asked if I could make time for a dinner date that week. I said that

the calendar was jam-packed and that it would be tough to squeeze anything else in. He told me that it was all right, and that he knew I would do my best.

... That's a perfect place for dialogue.

Passages like the one above *tell* readers what was said, instead of *showing* them—and, as we've learned, showing is almost always more effective than telling.

Here is a better way to convey this conversation:

> "Honey, could we make time for a dinner date this week?"
>
> "Not sure. My schedule's packed right now."
>
> "No problem. I know you'll do your best."

Not only is dialogue easier to read on the page, it allows your readers to *imagine* the speakers standing in the kitchen, and gives a sense of their speaking voices.

Once you write out what was said, and by whom, you can add visual cues or internal actions to the dialogue, so you can show both what is said, and what is not said.

This is where things really get juicy. You can use the same dialogue to convey any number of different emotions, simply by changing the cues around it!

Here's the distracted couple:

> "Honey, could we make time for a dinner date this week?"
>
> "Not sure," I answered, scrolling through the calendar on my phone. "My schedule's packed right now."
>
> He shrugged, and went back to rummaging in the fridge. "No problem. I know you'll do your best."

Here's the fighting couple:

"Honey, could we make time for a dinner date this week?"

"Not sure," I answered flatly, scrolling through my online calendar so I wouldn't have to look at him. "My schedule's packed right now."

He sighed, "No problem." Then, in a voice dripping with irony, he added, "I know you'll do your best."

And here's the regretful but happy couple:

"Honey, could we make time for a dinner date this week?"

"Not sure." I sighed, slumping against the counter. "My schedule's packed right now."

He wrapped me in his arms, and kissed my hair. "No problem. I know you'll do your best."

Each of these simple examples conveys a totally different energy—not only through the dialogue, but through the actions around it. These are the *visual cues* that give context to the conversation, and add drama and emotion to the dialogue.

He Said, She Said

Many novice dialogue writers get caught in the "he said, she said" trap, and feel that they have to add some version of the word "said" to every line of dialogue.

"Honey," he asked, "Could we make time for a dinner date later this week?"

"Not sure," I answered. "My schedule's packed right now."

"No problem," he replied. "I know you'll do your best."

This is unnecessary, and distracts from the actions and emotional cues around the dialogue. Since it's clear after the first line who is speaking, there is no need to remind readers who is who. Nor is there a need to insert synonyms for "said" like *asked, answered, retorted,* or *stated.* Instead, supplement the dialogue with actions—but again, not too many, and only those actions which convey the energy and emotions you want readers to take away from the dialogue.

In long sections of dialogue—especially dialogue between only two people (as opposed to a group)—you should only use "said" words and action cues as often as needed to clarify who is speaking and keep the action moving forward. If you need a quantitative guide, every five to six lines is usually adequate.

More Tips For Writing Effective Stories

- *Write all stories from your own perspective, even if they belong to someone else.* Unless you are using testimonials which were actually written by your clients or study participants, and separating them in the layout so that they are self-contained, don't try to write other people's stories from the "I" perspective. Since you are already using your own voice throughout the rest of the book, adding another first-person viewpoint can confuse your readers. Also, because the first-person perspective gives your readers access to the thoughts and feelings of the narrator, writing someone else's story this way requires a heavy dose of inference, which can lead to inaccuracies.

- *Don't skimp on details, because readers are nosy.* Invoking emotion is definitely the most important part of storytelling, but if you hold back too many details about events and relationships, your readers will get frustrated. They want to know what happens, just as much as they want to know how you felt about it.

- *Be sure that all of the action you include is significant to the overall point of your story.* If anything feels extraneous, or doesn't illustrate your point, remove it.

- *Take all story arcs to their conclusion.* You are not writing a fictional murder mystery, so don't put in any cliffhangers. If you tell the story of how Aunt Betty's stroke forced you to reassess your priorities, please, for goodness' sake, tell us what happened to Aunt Betty, too! Did she recover? How did the drama resolve? (See the note on details above.)

- *Learn how to craft good fiction.* Although you are sharing true stories, basic fiction writing techniques—like characterization, dialogue, and emotional hooks—can and should be applied. (I've included some of my favorite reference books in the Resources section.)

How much story is too much?

Well, it depends. Stories aren't facts, so if your book is research-dependent, you will need to balance your stories or case studies with statistics and explanations. However, for most inspirational books, I would say that there can *never* be too many stories, as long as every story adds some new piece of information or insight for readers. After all, not every reader is going to relate powerfully to every story in your book (although, if you write your stories well, they will relate at least a little bit to every single one); therefore, the more stories you have, the greater the chance of your readers "getting it."

If you feel like your book is too story-heavy, ask yourself the following questions about each of your "extra" stories:

- Does this story introduce a new concept, illustrate a new point, or reveal some other information which is vital to readers' connection, understanding, or transformation?

- Is this story necessary for readers to understand other stories that come later in the book?
- Does this story move the overall narrative forward?
- Is this story emotionally relatable to my readers?
- Why am I attached to including this story?

Here's a good rule of thumb. If your stories are short and sweet (read, under two pages long) it is perfectly fine to use two or three to make a point or illustrate a concept. After all, multiple viewpoints increase your readers' chance of understanding. However, if your story is longer or more involved, it should stand alone so it can make the maximum emotional impact.

Finally, don't be afraid to swap out your stories. Your first draft (and second draft) are all about playing, so experiment with multiple versions of multiple stories. Write from different angles and starting points. Add new emotions, (and their attendant actions, dialogue, and visual cues), and take others out. You may be surprised by what works!

TEACHING VOICE VS. STORY SHARING VOICE

There is—and should be—a difference between how we share stories and how we give instructions to readers.

When you share stories in a book, you are sharing *confidences*, and your tone and word choices should reflect this. Also, as I mentioned earlier, you will want to write your stories from your own perspective—and that means sharing your intimate thoughts, feelings, and insights with your readers.

Once your stories are told, you will likely shift the narrative to a discussion or analysis of the "heart" of the story, and what you want readers to learn from it. (I'll share more about how to do this in Chapter 5.) This shift in focus will also necessitate a shift in voice—from story-sharing voice to *teaching voice*.

Teaching voice is what I call the "you" perspective. You are speaking directly to your readers, just as you would in a face-to-face conversation. During this conversation, you will likely make observations, give instructions, and provide information that readers can use to create the outcome you have promised.

Chances are, you will recognize the teaching voice from just about every self-help book, blog post, or how-to you've ever read. It probably feels natural for you to write in this way, because you've had practice elsewhere—and if so, that's great!

"But," you ask, "if teaching voice is so innate to non-fiction writing, why bother mentioning it at all?"

Because teaching voice, in most cases, does not mix well with storytelling.

That is not to say that the two can't coexist; Stephen King, for example, is masterful at integrating side conversations with readers into his story narratives. However, unless it is done well and consistently from the beginning of the book, interrupting a story with comments or instructions in teaching voice has the effect of pulling readers out of the emotion of the story, and dropping them into a new and unexpected conversation. Therefore, in most cases, you will want to finish telling your story *before* you dissect it for your readers.

If there is a part of the story that requires extra attention, quote it in your post-story discussion. That way, readers get to enjoy the story, and receive a verbatim reminder when it's time to get down to learning.

HOW TO WRITE ABOUT PEOPLE YOU KNOW

One of the questions I hear often is, "How can I ethically and responsibly tell stories about people I know?"

Obviously, the best answer to this question is, "Get their permission, and ask them to help you write their story."

I will also add, "Ask your story subjects to sign release forms before your book is published." Signed consent forms will protect you in the event that someone you have interviewed changes his or her mind after the book has been published.

However, in practice, obtaining consent isn't always possible. Maybe the person is no longer living. Maybe you haven't spoken to the person in years, and you don't want to re-open those lines of communication. Maybe you're revealing a dark family secret that you have kept hidden since childhood.

Does this mean that you can't write your story? Of course not. But it *does* mean that you should tread carefully, and treat the story (and the people involved) with respect and care.

Most people, when writing stories about actual events, are concerned about libel suits.

> **Libel:** \ˈlī-bəl\: *The act of publishing a false statement that causes people to have a bad opinion of someone.*

The operative words in that definition are "false statement." If you can provide proof that what you have written is true, you will automatically in a better situation.

It is also worth noting that libel only applies to the living, so if you are writing about someone who has passed on, you have a bit more leeway. However, since stories touch many lives, consider any others who may be injured by your story—especially if you are unclear about their roles in important events, or ascribe them untrue motivations.

Here are some broad guidelines for stories that feature other people who have not given you explicit permission to write about them:

- *Change or omit identifying details.* Not only names, but also physical features, locations, professions, and (in very delicate cases) some details of the actual events. Basically, a stranger should not be able to identify the person in question by researching your history or reading your Facebook page.

- *Write only what is true.* Even little white lies, if they defame the character of a real person, can be considered libel. Avoid the temptation to exaggerate for additional drama, and stick to the facts (minus names, places, and identifying details, of course).

- *Focus on how you felt, rather than what happened.* You can still create drama while holding back identifying facts about timelines and events. Just be sure that you are sharing enough to satisfy readers' curiosity!

- *If you're uncertain in any way, research libel law or consult a lawyer.* If someone cries libel, it is up to them to prove that you have intentionally defamed them. In cases where there are police records or other objective evidence of their wrongdoing, there is no way they can say it didn't happen, so you may be protected. But if you are writing about internal events in your marriage, family abuses that you have kept secret until now, or other events which, once revealed, may have a significant negative impact on the subject's life (or on the lives of those surrounding the subject), you will want to tell your stories in a way that won't come back to haunt you.

MOVING ON

You've finished writing your first draft, and taken steps to hone your story elements so that they really inform, engage, and excite your readers.

Now, it's time to move on to the next stage of your writing process, where you will start to refine your rough draft, and see the first glimmer of an awesome book start to peek through.

It's time to commence with Draft Two.

chapter 5

SHAPING THE CLAY

Your Second Draft

Y ou've done it! You've written your entire first draft!

You have officially passed the point where 90 percent of wannabe authors give up. You have busted through your excuses, guided yourself through the treacherous swamp of writer's block, and filled in each and every portion of your outline.

Take five minutes right now to do a happy dance.

No, I'm serious. Get up, right now. Congratulate yourself. Give yourself the credit you deserve, and a hearty pat on the back. (If I were there, I'd give you a great big hug.)

Then, when you're done celebrating, come back and meet me here, because there is still a lot to do to make your book the best it can be.

If you were a potter, I would say that you have just finished mixing your clay. You have a big lump of words and pages to work with, and now it needs to be carefully drawn out of itself, molded and coaxed into its most beautiful and potent form.

Your second draft is all about shapes: the overall shape of your book, including story arcs and your book's purpose and mission; and the smaller shapes of your chapters, subchapters, and sections. If you proceed with care and attention to detail, the smaller shapes of your sections and subchapters will nestle seamlessly into the larger shape of the book, like stackable mixing bowls or Russian nesting dolls.

So as you spin your metaphorical potter's wheel, you will need to balance your attention between the macro and micro views: your vision of the finished product, and the piece of the puzzle you currently have in your hands. This takes practice, patience, and a willingness to make mistakes—but luckily, I have created some processes to spare your brain the dizziness of tackling multiple viewpoints at once.

SECOND DRAFT STEP #1
TAKE A BREAK

Wait, what?

If it has been less than seven days since you finished your first draft, I applaud your diligence. Good for you for showing up so strongly after passing that first hurdle. However, I'm going to burst your bubble, and recommend that you set your first draft aside for at least a week before you begin your second draft.

Why? Because your brain needs recuperation time!

When you started your book creation process, you were in analytical mode. You determined your purpose and vision, and established the structure of your outline. Then, you switched to creative mode to free-write and create your first draft. Now, it is time to revert to that analytical mindset again, so that you can take the necessary steps to refine your draft without feeling overwhelmed or running yourself in circles.

Taking a short break of five to seven days between drafts allows you to view your book with fresh eyes. It also gives you time to untangle your emotions from your creative process—which in turn cuts down on internal resistance when it comes time to make your changes. During this break, use your designated writing practice time to work on other projects, or journal about the triumphs and struggles of writing your first draft.

Don't be tempted to set your draft aside for longer than two weeks, however. You don't want to lose the momentum you've created, or distance yourself too much from the energy of your book. If you feel strongly that you need more time away in order to be able to view your first draft objectively, be sure to keep your energetic connection to your book alive in other ways, such as re-reading your research notes, creating a cover mock-up, or working on your marketing copy.

Once you are ready to get started on your second draft, take a few moments to sit quietly and align yourself again with your purpose and mission. Re-read your Purpose Statement and your outline. Tap into the excitement you felt when you first created your book concept. Then, open Chapter 1, and get started.

SECOND DRAFT STEP #2
THE FIRST READ-THROUGH

The first thing you should do when beginning your second draft is to read your first draft from beginning to end.

Try to come to it with a "beginner's mind"—that is, without opinions or expectations, as if you weren't the one who wrote it.

As you read, keep your outline and a notebook handy. Take notes on your draft, and ask questions—but don't change anything yet. This isn't a critique, or an edit: you are simply getting a bird's eye view of the landscape of your book.

Here are some things to ask/observe when conducting your initial read-through:

- What about this section/chapter do I love?
- What about this chapter feels "off"?
- Are there any elements in this chapter/section that deviate from my established chapter template?
- Are there any areas where the tone or energy of the narrative changes substantially?

- Does my material in each section answer the questions I intended to address, as noted in my outline?

- In each chapter and/or section, are the solutions I'm offering clearly presented?

- Are there any hanging storylines, unfinished sections, or other hard breaks in the narrative?

- Are there any sections that would benefit from more discussion, explanation, or story?

- Are my action steps complete and easy to follow?

- When I've referenced concepts or sections in other parts of the book, are my references accurate and easy to identify? (Remember, a one-sided reference is a broken promise—so if you wrote "We'll talk more about this later," or "We will explore this concept in Chapter 5," be sure that readers can find that piece of information easily.)

As you read, also note any creative insights you receive. Sometimes, re-reading your draft will trigger a story or memory that you had forgotten, or prompt you to create a new exercise for your readers. Jot down everything that jumps into your thought field, no matter how big or small. You can decide later whether to actually include these ideas; remember, right now you are just getting the big picture.

Once you have read your entire draft and made notes on all the places where your content needs work (there will be many, so don't let it throw you), it will be time to go back to the beginning, ask some pointed questions, and actually make those changes. You may need to rewrite certain sections to work the necessary information into your narrative, and that is perfectly okay. In fact, it is sometimes better to completely rewrite a section to flow smoothly than to cut and paste paragraphs and try to make the current wording fit. Remember, you are shaping your clay—and sometimes, even a master potter has to squish her vase down into a lump and start over.

SECOND DRAFT STEP #3
ASK THE TOUGH QUESTIONS

Working with your second draft is very much akin to your personal development process. Your first draft was like your teenage years, when you were just forming your ideas and putting it all out there. Your second draft is like your thirties; now that you have a clearer perspective and more experience, you can edit, revise, and reposition major parts of your life and identity by asking, "What belongs, and what doesn't?"

While re-reading and reworking your draft, you will inevitably come across places that feel like they don't quite fit. Maybe the narrative goes off on a tangent, or loops back upon itself. In places, you might find yourself thinking, "I've read this before, haven't I?"

(Yup. Just like life.)

Reworking your draft can be every bit as uncomfortable as personal development work, too. Now that you have identified your book's potential trouble spots, it is time to go back and start asking those tough questions about every piece of content that raised a flag for you—and even those that did not.

Here are some questions to ask about each piece of your material:

- Does this portion of content really serve my readers, as well as the overall mission and purpose of my book?

- Is this the energy I want this content to embody, or is there a better way to frame this?

- Does this section give readers a piece of the answer to my overall question or chapter question?

- Will readers care about this story? Why or why not?

You may find it hard to let go of certain parts of your writing. This is normal and natural. After all, you have created something, and now you might need to unmake it. (See the section on attachment later in this chapter.) Just don't let your resistance stop you from making changes that will ultimately benefit the book.

Here are some additional questions to help you determine if those "iffy" pieces belong in your book:

- Does this material directly support, reinforce, or answer a question about the topic of this chapter or section? If not, ask:
    - How can I rework this so that it directly supports my chapter and subchapter topics?
    - Is there somewhere else in the book where this information would fit more easily?
- Have I made this point before? If so, do I need to repeat it now? (See the section on reiteration, below.)
- What is the ultimate benefit of this particular material to readers?
- Do I actually need this information at all?

When to Reiterate

A common question I hear from writers in the review stage is "When and how often should I repeat my key points?"

Many popular self-help authors repeat themselves frequently throughout their books. Ostensibly, this ensures that readers recall the necessary information from previous sections to get the most out of the topic at hand. However, when reiteration is used in a heavy-handed way, it can feel patronizing, like the book has been "dumbed down."

I've read many well-regarded books where the writer repeated him- or herself over and over to make a point, or used the same catchphrase on every page. It got to the point where I was skimming because I knew exactly what was coming. Believe me, you don't want readers to skip over large sections of your book because they're bored!

With some trial and error, you will find a healthy balance between providing helpful nudges and beating readers senseless.

Repetition should be used as a tool to assist your readers; therefore, consider the following:

- What are the two or three "big truths" of which I want readers to remain aware at all times?
- What is the approximate number of pages I expect my readers to consume in a single sitting?
- What are the learning traits of my ideal readers? Do they need lots of hand-holding, or will they remain more engaged if they have to intentionally revisit my core concepts?
- What level of repetition will best compliment my tone and the overall energy of the book?
- When I read a book, what level of repetition do I find helpful?

Your "big truths" are the foundational principles on which your teaching is based. They will relate to the outcome you intend for your readers, but may not match it exactly. For example, if your book is about manifestation, one of your Big Truths might be, "We all have the power to change our reality." Such core principles will bear repeating at least a few times over the course of the book.

The number of pages you expect your readers to consume is important because you will want to offer "refreshers" at the points where someone might naturally stop (and start) reading. That way, readers aren't inundated with too many reminders in a single sitting, but are able to reconnect quickly when they pick up your book again.

Your ideal readers and overall tone determine your level of repetition because they also influence your teaching style. A "nurturing" book will probably include more coaxing and gentle reminders than a book which challenges readers to become free-thinking mavericks.

Finally, knowing your own preferences keeps things true to your energy and intention.

Here are some helpful ways to use repetition:

- To remind readers of one or more of your "big truths" before introducing a new layer of information.
- To prompt readers to recall a lesson they learned two or three chapters prior, so that it is fresh in their minds when you introduce a new concept.
- To refresh readers' memories after a natural "break" in the narrative, at which point they may have put down the book.

Here are some places *not* to use repetition:

- After every story or case study. You want the current teaching point to be crystal clear, but there is no need to remind readers about what was discussed earlier in the current chapter—or, if your chapters are short, in the prior chapter.
- Within every section or chapter. Even if you are referencing the "big truths" of your book, constant repetition can make readers feel patronized.

How to reiterate successfully:

- Use a new approach. Remember our Crystal Clause exercise from Chapter 3? You can use this technique to help you repeat your "big truths" in different ways throughout the book. Sometimes, readers need to hear the same thing in a different way.
- Add new tidbits each time. Each time you reinforce a concept, add a bit of new information or perspective. Build on what you have said before.

SECOND DRAFT STEP #4
PATCH THE POTHOLES

Sometimes, at this point in your book's evolution, the road to your book's promised outcome can look a little ... rough.

If your book's path feels any less smooth than a superhighway, you will want to patch the potholes and create a smooth, even ride from start to finish in each section, and across the whole book—in other words, fill in any missing information, and be sure that your existing information is clear, concise, and polished.

In your initial read-through, you assessed whether your content fully answered the questions posed in each section and chapter. Anywhere you added notes about how to better answer a question is a place that could benefit from additional material.

You can also add new material to any of the places where new ideas were sparked in your read-through. However, it is vital to think critically about your additions, and consider the points below, before you start tweaking your narrative. Overall, your new material must work in the greater context of the book, add new ideas or information, and be relevant to readers.

When *not* to add new material:

- When it repeats something that you already explored in a previous section or chapter, without introducing new concepts.

- When it supports a point you have made elsewhere but doesn't fully support the point you are making in the current section.

- When it upsets the balance and flow of a chapter, and/or makes one particular chapter substantially longer than the others.

- When it leads readers off on a tangent, and away from the logical flow of your Information Delivery System.

Eliminate Circular Reasoning

If you find an instance of circular reasoning in your narrative, you will also have discovered a great place to add new material.

Circular reasoning is the act of using the same idea as both an argument and its conclusion. It assumes that, if the premise of the argument is true, then the conclusion must also be true, and subsequently attempts to "win" the argument by repeating the initial statement in different, often progressively strengthening terms.

In other words, circular reasoning is using the "truth" you are presenting to justify itself.

Please don't misunderstand: the issue is not that your ideas are wrong until proven otherwise. It's simply that circular reasoning is not an effective tool for changing readers' beliefs or mindsets. Since it assumes itself to be "right" from the get-go, it effectively shuts out any energy with which it is not already aligned.

Here are two simple examples of circular reasoning:

> "I have something important to say, so you should let me talk."

And another, using our Crystal Clause exercise from Chapter 3 (because, again, Crystal Clauses say the same thing in different ways).

> "No problem exists that cannot be solved with love; therefore, love is the answer to everything."

Circular reasoning appears more often in inspirational writing than you might think. When writing in a "new-age" or inspirational field, many authors mistakenly assume that their readers will already be familiar with certain concepts; and, more, that they will believe those concepts to be true. This is not always the case.

While an argument designed to introduce a "newbie" to your way of thinking may feel repetitive to readers who have more experience with your topic, learning the basics again (and from a new perspective) never hurt anyone.

Therefore, when in doubt, explain yourself.

When we utilize circular reasoning in discussion, it is generally because a.) we believe the statement to be true and assume that our readers will agree, or b.) we believe the statement to be true, but haven't taken the time to think through the reasons *why* we believe it. Both can be solved by explaining the process by which we arrived at the conclusion in question.

For example, instead of the Crystal Clause example on the previous page, we might write, "Every time I tried to solve a problem in anger, I only made it worse. Eventually, I had to concede that there might be a better solution. That's when love found me."

Yes, this is still opinion, but it shows a basic development of thought which doesn't rely on the assumption that the idea itself is infallible.

If you can't find a story or process to illustrate your argument and remove the circular reasoning, or if nothing in your direct experience supports your conclusions, it might be time to reassess your stance.

SECOND DRAFT STEP #5
HONE YOUR DISCUSSION SECTIONS

Let's say that you have shared a story about how one of your clients found and maintained inner peace throughout a series of challenging events, including the passing of her father. The story focuses on the actions, reactions, thoughts, and feelings of the main character (your client) as she moves through this particular portion of her life.

You have shown readers how your client sat by her father's bedside as he took his last breaths, and how her deep, steady breathing calmed everyone in the room. You have shown her feelings of gratitude for her father's life, and some of the actions she took to express that gratitude. And, in the last scene of the story, you've shown your client walking out of the hospital with a smile on her face, filled with joy that she'd been blessed with such an amazing dad.

It's a great story, and you're pretty proud of it. But what, exactly, is it teaching?

This is where your discussion comes in.

While re-reading your draft, you may have noticed that there isn't always an obvious association between your stories and the point you are trying to make. (Or maybe you hadn't noticed it, but now I've got you thinking about it!)

In Chapter 4, we clarified that, in most cases, you shouldn't try to integrate teaching voice or asides to readers in your stories. Pausing to reflect in the middle of a story can fragment the plot and muddy the narrative. However, once the story is over, and readers are emotionally invested, you can freely explore all of the teaching points that the story presents.

This post-story text is your *discussion*, and it is one of the best places to teach readers the key lessons of your book.

When analyzing the vital components of a story for your readers, it is best to be totally, excruciatingly clear—like, "Boom! Here's what I want you to learn!" Don't assume that because the teaching point is obvious to you, it will be obvious to everyone. You are coming from a place of already knowing, while at least a portion of your readers will be brand new to your subject and material. What seems simple to you may be a revelation to others.

Here are some helpful questions to ask about your discussion to ensure that readers get the most out of your stories:

- What is my primary objective for this story? (What do I want readers to take away from this story?)
- Have I stated my primary objective clearly in the discussion?
- Have I stated any other teaching points (secondary objectives) clearly in the discussion?
- Have I illustrated my teaching elements from multiple angles? If so, is each angle fully explained?

Since your teaching stories already focus on the events, emotions, and energies that are most closely tied to your purpose, vision, and desired reader outcome, this process should feel fairly straightforward. It's really a matter of honing the discussion so that your readers get the most possible benefit from the story.

The PIE Method

After the story is finished (and your readers are hooked), your discussion will invite them to consider the themes and lessons of the story and how they can apply them to their own experience. The goal of your discussion is to elicit "lightbulb moments" for your readers, using persuasive writing that moves them from emotion to understanding.

One highly effective way to do this is to use the PIE Method.

PIE is an acronym for "Point (or Primary Objective), Illustration, Explanation." This method of paragraph development is widely used in academia but also applies beautifully to conversational writing.

For example, after concluding the example story from the previous section, you might open your discussion with a statement like:

> Mary's story proves that it is possible to find and maintain inner peace, even in the most painful circumstances.

This is your *point*, or primary objective; it tells readers what you want them to learn from the story.

Next, refer to specific points in the story that *illustrate* your point and support your assertion, like this:

> When Mary stepped back from her own grief and anger and allowed herself to just be with her father, not only was she able to feel more peaceful, she was able to broadcast that energy of calm throughout the entire room.

Then, *explain* how readers can create the same results in their own lives (and take a step toward the outcome you have promised.)

> When we fully accept what is real *right now*—without fighting it, denying it, or blaming others for it—we can find the peace that lives within us. From that safe and empowered place, we can move forward deliberately, knowing that, inside us, all is well. How do we get to that place of acceptance? First, we need to understand why we fight our reality in the first place.

Which, of course, brings us to the next paragraph, and the next set of teaching points (for which you can also utilize the PIE method).

Formatting your discussion according to the PIE method allows you to explore your teaching points in a way that feels logical and easy to relate to.

Other Ways to Highlight Your Teaching Points

Besides the PIE method, there are other ways to draw out the teaching elements in your stories. Not all of them will work for you in every situation, but they are still great tools to have in your toolkit.

The Preemptive Statement

Another construction common in academic writing is to state the primary objective of the discussion before presenting the substantiating information (or, in this case, the story).

For example, before sharing the example story from the last section, you might write something like:

> In the following story, you will see how Mary was able to maintain her inner peace through a set of devastating circumstances, including the death of a loved one.

I call this a *preemptive statement.*

Personally, I prefer not to use preemptive statements for key stories (by which I mean the central stories of each chapter or section), because they narrow your readers' viewing angle. The difference between opening a section with the story itself and opening with a preemptive statement is the difference between asking someone to find the lone birch tree in a landscape photo, and simply circling the tree in red ink. The first way sets readers a task; the second simply tells them where to look.

The same goes for introducing your stories. If you use a preemptive statement, readers will scan the story for the parts which support your primary objective, rather than taking in the story as a whole. If this is okay with you, that's great—but keep in mind that any story you share, as long as it is well-constructed, will probably spark a number of connections in your readers, not all of which you can anticipate. In such cases, telling them what to look for can be counterproductive.

On the other hand, preemptive statements can be quite helpful for "supporting" stories—shorter, secondary stories that repeat or reframe the lessons of the key story. Because you have already told the key story, and shared your thoughts on it via the discussion section, an objective statement before the supporting story simply serves to remind readers to look for the lessons.

For example, after your discussion of Mary's story and your analysis of the vital teaching points, you might introduce a secondary story with an preemptive statement.

> Like Mary, Shane was hit with hurricane force by a series of life events. However, his experience of inner peace came not only from acceptance of his circumstances, but from the discovery that he had the power to change those circumstances by making different choices.

Then, when you launch into Shane's story, your readers will be prepared to look for both the similarities and the differences between Mary's story and Shane's.

Multiple Viewpoints

Use multiple viewpoints in your discussion to highlight questions that readers might have about the story, and introduce new teaching points.

For example, you might write something like:

> When Mary first told me her story, I was amazed by the fact that she was able to maintain her inner peace through her father's death. "How solid must her connection be to herself," I wondered, "for her to maintain her calm through such an ordeal?"
>
> However, when I told Mary's story to my friend Jill, her response was quite different. "She must have been totally repressing her grief," Jill commented. "Maybe she was peaceful in the moment, but did it really serve her in the long run?"

Jill's reaction to Mary's story is the perfect opening to a secondary line of discussion. It also validates a concern that many of your readers might share.

You don't need to get reactions to your key stories from a dozen different sources to integrate multiple viewpoints effectively. However, it may be helpful to ask one or two trusted friends to give feedback. (Just on the stories, mind you, not the whole chapter. That comes later, after you have finished your second draft.)

If for some reason feedback is not possible, you can invent—carefully and sparingly—multiple viewpoints based on the questions you feel readers will ask.

SECOND DRAFT STEP #6
CLARIFY YOUR ACTION STEPS

If you have included action steps in your chapters—aka, how-tos, instructions, tips, or practices—you will want to take this opportunity to refine them and check them against your narrative.

Before you ask them to take an action step, readers should understand three things:

- *How* to take the step you are advising.
- *Why* this action step is vital to the result you promise.
- *When* they should take this step.

The "How"

Make sure that your readers have the tools they need to take the action step. This means that, if the action step advises them to "romance their inner critics," the narrative and/or story discussion should provide all of the information they require to do so effectively.

The "Why"

No one wants to waste time doing exercises that don't advance their goals. Make sure that the "why" of your action steps is clear in your narrative. You can also offer a quick one-paragraph refresher before your action steps if you feel that the stories and/or discussion weren't enough.

The "When"

Make sure that your action steps are presented in a linear order. When readers get to an action step, they should already have completed all of the necessary "prep work" to be able to succeed with the current assignment.

SECOND DRAFT STEP #7
RELEASE YOUR ATTACHMENTS

You have been working with your draft for a while now, and have probably noticed that you are a teensy bit ... attached to your prose.

Maybe you wrote a passage that feels really eloquent, but doesn't flow with the material around it. Maybe you have created a story that, while slightly off-topic, feels too powerful to delete. You want to make sure these gems stay intact, so you skew the surrounding narrative to accommodate them.

However, this tendency to nurture certain passages or paragraphs can weaken the rest of your book, because it knocks your book's purpose and vision out of your mental top-priority spot.

There is a (quite horrible) axiom that is commonly applied to fiction writing. You may have heard it: "Kill your darlings." It means that, quite often, the parts of your writing to which you are most attached are the ones you need to cut.

I agree with this, but conditionally. Pride in beautiful prose is not a bad thing. In fact, you may surprise yourself with the words that pour out of you during your creation process. However, when that attachment or pride gets in the way of the greater purpose of your book, it becomes a liability.

Here's a blunt truth:

> *Not everything you created in your first draft will make it into the final version of your book!*

Most of the time, I end up keeping only around 60 percent of what I write in a first draft!

In your creative process, you are going to get sidetracked, run away with tangents, or place emphasis where it isn't needed. Even if you stuck to your outline like glue while writing your first draft, there will be elements in your narrative that just don't pass muster.

Here are some common "darlings" that should be subjected to a relevance test.

- The story that doesn't offer anything new to readers.
- The metaphor or simile that doesn't make a new point or offer new information.
- The sentence that says the same thing as a previous sentence, only in a "prettier" way.
- The well-worded instance of circular reasoning. (Eloquence does not an argument make!)

The Relevance Test (aka, The Cut Test)

One way to determine if your darlings are actually contributing to your book is to subject them to a cut test.

Create a "cut sections" file or folder. Then, put on your mad scientist cap, and subject your "darlings"—and any other questionable passages, paragraphs, or sentences—one by one to the following experiment.

- Cut and paste the section in question into your "cut sections" file. Hit the "save" button.
- Walk away for five minutes. Meditate, do some deep breathing, or make a cup of tea.
- Come back and read your draft again, minus the cut section.
- Ask yourself: "Does this read better without the cut section? Is it clearer, and more to the point?"

If the answer to the last question is "yes," leave your darling in the "cut sections" file and proceed to the next item on your list. If the answer is "no," reincorporate *only* the elements of your cut section which enhance readers' understanding of the teaching point.

When you find yourself caught up in a romance with your darlings, it is helpful to remind yourself that you aren't writing this book for *you*. Oh, it will definitely serve you, in all kinds of ways—but the end product is not intended solely for your personal consumption. Therefore, it is vital to place clarity of communication over personal attachment.

Besides, those darlings might nestle quite well into your next book!

MOVING ON

Once you have gone through your entire draft, honed your stories, refined your teaching elements, perfected your action steps, and evaluated your attachments, you should have a fairly solid version of your book in hand.

Congratulations! You made it through the first round of revisions, and are now ready to tackle Draft 2.1!

Draft 2.1 (aka, Your Second Second Draft)

Essentially, this revision process is the same as the one you just went through, only up-leveled.

Once again, begin by setting your book aside for a few days. Then, do a read-through from beginning to end. Take notes on the places that still aren't quite where you want them to be, and go through your revision process with as much objectivity as possible.

Repeat the Second Draft action steps outlined in this chapter as many times as it takes for you to:

- Ensure that every section of your book, from start to finish, closely follows the flow of your Information Delivery System.

- Feel confident that each chapter follows a clear template and narrative path.

- Ensure that all questions posed in your outline and by your chapter and subchapter topics are answered completely by your stories, discussion sections, and other parts of the narrative.

- Remove any extraneous or tangential material.

- Support all stories, case studies, and interviews with discussion of teaching points.

- Give action steps that are 100 percent supported by the narrative and are easy for readers to follow.

- Feel at least 85 percent confident in every piece of your material.

Yes, 85 percent confident is all you need to feel.

Why? Because if I told you that you needed to feel 100 percent confident in your whole book, you would never move on to the next step! (Or, you'd pull a fake-it-till-you-make-it move, and possibly skip over some really juicy revisions.)

When you have completed Draft 2.1 (or 2.2, or 2.6, as the case may be), and have done everything humanly possible to make your content the best it can be, it will be time to take a leap of faith, let go of your fears, and *ask for feedback.*

part 3

polish & refine

Chapter 6

EXPANDING THE CIRCLE

How to Ask For and Receive Feedback

"W hat?" You exclaim. "I have to ask other people to read my book? But it's not even finished!"

No, you're not finished. You still have your entire third draft (aka, your self-edit) to complete. But you didn't think you were going to write your book in a vacuum, did you?

Why Feedback Is Important

Unless you intend to keep your book in a drawer and never publish it, you are writing for an *audience*. Therefore, it is vital to know how that audience is going to respond to your book, and take steps to improve that response so that as many readers as possible will achieve the results you've promised.

It's time to call upon your *beta readers*.

Writers need beta readers for the same reason that plays need directors. You need someone who will see what the audience sees, and give you clues about how to improve the performance. When you are the lead actor on the stage, your dialogue is delivered through all of your mental filters, and enhanced by all of your knowledge and experience. You know what you are saying, and where it is leading, and how the scene ends. However, you can't see or hear yourself as others see or hear you. You can't be on the stage and in the stands at the same time.

In other words, *you can't have a reader's experience with your own book*, so you need to ask for help from people who can.

I know, perhaps better than most, how scary it can be to ask for feedback. Not only have I been through the process numerous times myself, I've coached dozens of writers through it. And, I'm sorry to say, if you have confidence issues, are averse to being "wrong," or are scared of being judged, this part of the process *will* bring up those issues.

However, learning to ask for and receive feedback is one of the most important things you can do for yourself, both as a writer and as a human being. In this chapter, I will teach you what you need to know to not only receive feedback gracefully, but actually grow from it.

Why is feedback important now?

To me, the best time to ask for feedback is after you have finished your content but before you do your line edits and proofreading.

Why? Because the information you receive through this process will prompt you to make changes, and some of them might be pretty major. There is no point in spending hours perfecting a section that will eventually be cut. (Remember my example from Chapter 3 about the wood carving?) Unless you are a natural editor, and actually enjoy picking apart sentence structure and nosing out unnecessary participles—in which case, more power to you!—you won't want to do more line edits than necessary. Also, the information your beta readers provide might influence your self-editing process as much or more than it does your content.

If you feel very strongly about giving your readers a draft that is as close to perfect as you can make it, you can ignore my advice, skip to Chapter 8, do your self-edits, and then come back and meet me here. Otherwise, run your spell check and fix any glaring errors, but don't worry about formatting or grammatical issues just yet.

FEEDBACK STEP #1
GATHER YOUR BETA TEAM

"Okay," you might be saying. "I understand why now is the perfect time to receive feedback, but how do I know whom to ask?"

There are many potential sources of feedback out there, most of whom can be grouped into one of three categories:

- *Amateur.* These include your friends, coworkers, mastermind colleagues, novice members of your writing group, and your family. Basically, they are people whose opinions you value, but who don't necessarily have any specific knowledge about writing a book.

- *Experienced.* People in this category are senior members of your writing group, other published authors, writing professors, and the like.

- *Professional.* These are people who actually work in the book industry, like professional editors, book coaches, literary agents, and publishers.

If you are not hiring an editor or a book coach, and don't already have an agent, you should ask a minimum of three capable, trustworthy people in the Amateur and Experienced categories to review your manuscript. These people should be avid readers, come from diverse backgrounds, and have at least some knowledge (tutored or untutored) about what makes a book readable, effective, and persuasive. Ideally, they should also represent a broad range of experience with your subject matter—from deeply immersed in your subject to no knowledge at all.

Before you start handing out your book, however, take some time to sit with your choices. Just because someone looks like a good beta reader doesn't mean s/he will be able to give you feedback you can actually accept. The way in which you relate, emotionally and energetically, to your beta readers is every bit as important as their on-paper qualifications.

So, ask yourself the following questions about every potential beta reader *before* approaching him or her to review your book:

- Do I trust this person?
- Can I be vulnerable with this person?
- Can I debate constructively with this person?
- Can this person be objective about me and my work?
- Does this person understand my goals and vision for this book?
- Do I respect this person's opinion and values?

No matter what someone's external qualifications are, they are no use to you as a beta reader if they communicate in a way that doesn't resonate with you, include personal attacks in their criticism, or hold a non-negotiable opposing stance to your goals, vision, or subject matter (hence the question about constructive debate).

At this point, you have probably narrowed the field of potential candidates substantially. Now, it is time to invite the people on your short list to play with you in the realm of book creation.

What if no one I know can do this for me?

If that's the case, ask for help! Put out a call through friends, social media, or your writers' group for qualified reviewers. Ask at your local college if there are writing students or junior professors who are willing to share their ideas. You won't know what's possible until you ask!

FEEDBACK STEP #2
PREPARE YOUR BETA READERS

Before you drop your manuscript on their doorsteps, it is a good idea to let your beta readers know exactly what the review process entails. That way, they can evaluate whether they can commit to the full amount of time and energy required.

Because reading and commenting on an entire book is no small undertaking, you may want to throw in some leverage, like a free copy of the book, a free coaching session, a gift certificate to their favorite restaurant ... whatever. Don't underestimate the value of reciprocity!

Here are some questions to ask your reviewers before they sign on:

- Do you have time to read this entire manuscript carefully and completely?
- Are you willing to answer a list of questions I provide, as well as make your own notes and comments as you read?
- Do you feel comfortable offering me honest, unfiltered feedback?
- Do you feel comfortable offering suggestions for how I can improve the manuscript?

If your reviewers are willing to go the distance, great! You have assembled your reviewing team. Now, it is time to outline their tasks and get them started.

Ask Powerful Questions, Get Powerful Feedback

How you ask for feedback directly determines the quality of the answers you will receive. Therefore, take the time to consider what you actually want to get out of this process—and then, make it easy for your beta readers to deliver the goods.

What are helpful questions?

Most people have no idea how to prep beta readers to provide actionable feedback on their writing, so they ask leading, too-general, or "closed" questions that fail to elicit the responses they are actually seeking.

Here are some examples of unhelpful questions:

- Did you like it? (Only invites a yes or no answer.)
- Do you think many people will buy this book? (Subjective. Chances are, your beta readers won't have any idea what the current marketplace looks like.)
- What is wrong with my book? (Invites only negative comments, which of course aren't helpful.)
- Do you think I'm a good writer? (Subjective and leading. You are obviously only after one answer.)

When you ask for feedback on your writing, be as specific as possible so that the responses can actually help you grow, rather than spinning you in circles.

The questions you pose to your beta readers should leave plenty of room for opinion, explanation, and constructive criticism.

In other words, tell them *what to look for*, not what to think.

This can feel vulnerable, because you are opening yourself up to a range of feedback, not all of which may be as glowing as you hope. However, asking specific questions creates a contained space for you to receive, process, and apply each piece of information. For example, a request to improve the clarity of one section feels much more approachable than a general comment like, "The book was okay, but you could use more clarity."

Create a checklist for your beta readers, and send it along with your book. Ask them to pay extra attention to your trouble spots (note the page numbers), or places where you feel the narrative is shaky. Ask them to assess your book's content based on the questions you posed in your outline and the overall question asked by the title and subtitle. Finally, request that they actually perform the practices or action steps in each chapter, and comment on the process.

In essence, ask them to *be* your ideal reader, and do what your ideal reader would do.

Here are some examples of general (aka, pertaining to the entire book) questions that you might ask your beta readers:

- What is your overall impression of the tone, vision, and energy of the book?

- In your opinion, how can I express my concept more clearly to someone who is new to my subject?

- Did you feel like the first chapters gave you all of the information you needed to get the most out of the rest of the book? If not, what questions came up for you as you read? Where did you feel you needed more information, explanation, or clarification?

- Do you think that my book followed through on the promise I made in the title/subtitle? Where did you feel you wanted/needed more information?

- Were there any places where the narrative felt out of alignment with the title and concept?

- Do you think that each chapter answered the question(s) or solved the problems posed at the beginning of the chapter? In which specific chapters did I do this well? In which specific chapters do I need to include more information?

- Do you feel that each chapter followed a logical, discernable format? Were you confused by the placement of any of the information – and if so, why?

- Did you notice any loose ends or unanswered questions in the stories?

- Were you able to connect to the stories/testimonials/ case studies I included, and were you invested in the outcome for the "characters?"

- Did the conclusion(s) I reached at the end of the book make sense to you? Why or why not?

- After reading the book, would you consider me an authority on my subject? If not, what information could I provide to shift that viewpoint?

- Did this book provide information that was of value to you in your everyday life? How will you apply your new knowledge going forward?

Next, here are some examples of more specific questions to ask about certain areas of content. (Obviously, you will want to adjust the questions below to be specific to your book.)

- In Chapter 3, did you feel that Story Subject A was a relatable character? Why or why not?

- When you did the exercises in Chapter 6, were you able to perform the meditation after reading it through once or twice, or did you have to keep opening your eyes to refer to the text?

- Will you actually implement any of the action steps in Chapter 10 in your own life? Why or why not?

- Do you think that the stories in Chapter 2 fully illustrated concepts X and Y? If not, what kinds of stories would more fully capture that concept for you?

- In your opinion, is Chapter 4 too long? Would the information be easier to digest if I broke it up into two chapters?

- Did you have enough background from Chapter 7 to fully understand the new information I presented in Chapter 8? If not, what else would you have liked to know before moving on?

- Does the story about my near-death-experience in Chapter 5 need more detail with regard to the accident? Do you have a complete picture of events leading up to the crash?

Finally, here are some questions about style, flow, and voice. These will guide you when you start working on your third draft. (Don't worry, I've provided all the tools you need to implement the answers to these questions, and more, in Chapter 8!)

- Is the writing clear and easy to read? If not, where did you struggle, and in what ways?

- In your opinion, was my writing voice strong and consistent throughout? If not, where can I adjust it?

- Did you connect to my writing voice? If not, what would make it more relatable to you?

- Did you notice any large or surprising variations in tone and/or word choices?

- Were there any places where my narrative seemed uncertain or apologetic (or, conversely, overly authoritative)?

- Did I use enough "reminders" or reiteration in the text to prompt you to recall information from previous section and chapters?

- Did I reiterate too often?

- Did you ever feel as though I was talking down to you?

- Did I repeat certain words, phrases, or metaphors multiple times? If so, do you have suggestions for replacing them?

- Were there any sentences or paragraphs that you had to re-read multiple times in order to understand?
- Did the narrative flow smoothly from section to section? If not, where did it feel choppy, and what are your suggestions for smoothing it out?

Notice that, whenever I've asked a yes-or-no question, I've also invited the beta reader to elaborate. This not only requires them to provide more information, it also prompts them to think critically about the text in order to formulate their answer, instead of just brushing off the question or answering in a general sense.

Play to Your Beta Readers' Strengths

Once you go through your manuscript and compile your list of questions, you may notice that you want your beta readers to look for issues in several categories, such as content and information flow, stories and characters, and grammatical issues.

Some beta readers may be capable of giving feedback in every category—and, if so, you should definitely take advantage of their talents. However, most will not, and that is perfectly okay. You will simply want to create questionnaires that play to each reader's strengths.

For example, if your friend Tilly is an amazing storyteller but couldn't pass a spelling test if her life depended on it, ask her to focus on things like character development and storylines, rather than sentence construction. Similarly, if your stepmom is a professor of classical literature and only reads books written before 1952, she will probably be great at dissecting your paragraphs, but may not be the best person to give you feedback on the applicability of your content.

If you use your questionnaires to direct your beta readers in a way that utilizes their greatest talents, you will end up with the greatest possible volume of useful feedback. Of course, you should invite your readers to offer insights outside the scope of what you have asked, but letting Tilly know that you aren't relying on her to check your spelling will likely make the process easier and more fun for her, as well as more helpful for you.

Once you have compiled your questionnaires, it will be time to send off your manuscript—so take a deep breath, say a prayer, and press "send."

By the time it comes back, you will be ready to get the most out of every answer.

FEEDBACK STEP #3
PREPARE YOURSELF TO RECEIVE FEEDBACK

Now that you have sent your manuscript off to your beta readers, it is time to prepare yourself to receive what they have to say.

Before we can receive feedback constructively, we must understand why criticism (or perceived criticism) of our writing hurts us so deeply.

Our creativity is inextricably tied to our sense of self. That's why, when someone critiques our work, or makes suggestions for its improvement, it feels like a shot to the heart. We feel as though our reviewer is telling *us* we need to change, or improve, or (gulp) be completely rewritten.

In order to learn from our mistakes and grow from constructive criticism (rather than running from it or retaliating against it), we need to remember that *what we produce does not define who we are.* Our work is simply a physical manifestation of our creative energy and intention, of which we have an abundant, even limitless, supply.

Our writing emerges *through* us, but we are so much more than the words we put on the page. Recognizing the places where we can grow doesn't make us *wrong* (or stupid, or incompetent, or any of the other labels our inner critics like to assign). Rather, it offers us an opportunity to channel our limitless creative energy through new and different pathways, and witness what happens as a result.

Becoming Receptive

When we shift our perspective to embrace the belief that we are more than what we create, we are able to assimilate feedback with greater ease, and even joy.

Embracing constructive feedback empowers us to learn more rapidly, since we are no longer wasting precious time and energy fighting against our reviewers (or our own egos). That learning, in turn, improves our focus, knowledge, and practical skills, which invigorate both our work and our confidence. And so the cycle goes.

Inner critics, though, love to get in the way of learning.

Your inner critic is the shadow side of your ego. It is the part of you that wants to remain in the safe zone of the known—which, in practice, means the lowest common denominator of your life—and which lashes out at anything that challenges that paradigm. It loves to remind you how small and unworthy you are, and can manipulate any information or situation to its own ends.

In order to be able to learn from feedback, you must first tame your inner critic. There are many ways to do this; in fact, entire books have been written on the subject. However, since I have limited page space in which to advise you, I will simply offer the approach which has always worked best for me.

When my inner critic lashes out in response to feedback, I pause, and ask my All-Purpose Power Question:

"What would it look like if…?"

What would it look like if I added this content? *What would it look like if* I played with this sentence's structure? *What would it look like if* I cut out the words my reviewer thinks are extraneous?

This question removes all absolutes. Suddenly, neither you nor your reviewers need to be "right" or "wrong," and the writing in question is not "good" or "bad." You are simply imagining a different approach, and playing with possibility as part of your creative process.

Now, doesn't that feel better?

Once you apply the All-Purpose Power Question, much of the feedback you receive will feel light and expansive. You will be able to see the advancements you can create in your work by incorporating your reviewers' suggestions, and get excited about implementing them. And if, after receiving all possibilities and outcomes with an open mind and heart, you honestly don't feel that the feedback will serve your book, you can set it aside without judgment.

When I started applying my All-Purpose Power Question to every piece of feedback, the outcome was threefold. First, I was able to get excited about feedback, because every piece of information felt like an exotic new country to explore. Second, I was able to actually train my inner critic to recognize possibility. Third, and most importantly, when my inner critic settled down to dissect the new possibilities in front of it, I was finally able to hear the quieter, but infinitely more powerful, voice of my creative soul.

Don't get me wrong, I still hear the snarky, doubting voice of my inner critic in my head sometimes. But now, I can think, feel, and imagine beyond it, because I know how to ask the questions that only my creative soul can answer.

If you have played with the All-Purpose Power Question, but can't feel the new possibilities because you feel fearful, angry, or locked-up inside, try working with the following meditation:

Meditation for Embracing Possibility

Imagine that you are a rosebud. Feel the many layers of protective petals wrapped around your heart, closed up tight. You can feel the sun on your outermost petals, but your core is shielded.

As you sit quietly, feel the sunlight warm you. This sun is the representation of your divine creative source, which always showers you with love. It will not burn you up, or dry you out.

Slowly, curiously, unfurl and extend your outermost petals. Let them bask in that warmth. Feel the golden light of the sun touch every part of those outer petals. Relax into the knowing that the sun will not harm you—that it will only illuminate you.

Then, unfurl your next layer of petals. Feel the expansive energy of this unfolding. Feel the tightness in your core start to ease as each layer of protection is softened.

After every layer of petals has fully opened, turn your face to the sun, and feel the radiant light of your divine creative source shimmering across every inch of your body. Feel the possibility inherent in this new state of being.

When you feel fully immersed in this openness, take seven deep breaths, and then open your eyes.

Weighing the Merit of Feedback

Imagine that you are learning to play the violin. You have been practicing one piece for a while, and you feel pretty proud of yourself. But when you play it for your teacher, he gently points out that you keep shifting your left hand to an awkward position, and it is making you play certain notes flat. Also, the note you've been reading as a high D is actually a D#.

Of course you feel deflated. You've been working on this piece for weeks! But if you argue with your teacher and tell him he's wrong, how will that help you stop playing flat notes? Also, a D# is a D#, and arguing about it will not change the note on the page to the one you like better.

My point is, some feedback is unquestionable. If a reviewer shares that you are using a word incorrectly, arguing with her will not change the word's definition. If she circles a misspelled word, your inner critic might pipe up with her usual rant about your grammatical incompetence, but that doesn't mean you shouldn't fix the word. (Instead, you could ask yourself, "*What would it look like if* I bought that grammar book Bryna recommended?")

Most feedback, however, is not absolute. It is based on *experience* and *opinion,* which are subjective in nature. This means that most feedback can't be immediately classified as correct or incorrect, because it is merely an observation based on your reviewer's *opinion of* and *experience with* your work.

Therefore, despite your reviewer's good intentions, the feedback may or may not actually serve the best interest of your book.

Sometimes, you can immediately see the merit in your reviewers' opinions (even if your inner critic doesn't like them). At these times, you should definitely use *"What would it look like if ...?"* to visualize the possibilities and act on them with excitement.

But other times, you may receive feedback that feels ... sticky. When that happens, you will need to rely on your inner wisdom to direct you.

If feedback feels sticky, it's probably because you're *resisting* it for one reason or another. Perhaps your inner critic is being sneaky, whispering over your shoulder instead of shouting in your face the way it usually does. Or, maybe the tone in which the feedback was delivered reminded you of a negative person in your life, and brought up all the attendant resentment. Either way, you may be tempted to discard the feedback altogether, because it feels too hard to process it objectively.

Try not to make a decision about "sticky" feedback until you've had time to examine your feelings carefully, and work with the All-Purpose Power Question. Sleep on it. Take a walk. Do what you need to do in order to calm your inner critic and separate your emotional associations from the information itself.

If you have managed to shush your inner critic for long enough to ask your questions, connect with your inner wisdom, and imagine the outcome of the feedback in question, and it *still* feels sticky, you have a decision to make. You can ask your reviewer to deliver the feedback from a different angle (so you can determine if it is simply a matter of approach), or you can ignore the feedback and move on.

Remember, *you are under no obligation to incorporate any of the feedback you receive.* If it honestly doesn't work for you, just leave it on the side of the road and keep moving toward your goal.

Before You Enter a Feedback Session

There are a number of ways to receive feedback, and you will want to explore all of them to see what works best for you.

In Person:

- *Pros:* You get to hear the tone and inflection, and see the body language, of the person giving feedback, instead of just reading his or her words. Also, you get to ask questions in real time and receive unscripted answers.

- *Cons:* If you tend to get emotional, or need extra time and space to process, this can feel more like an interrogation than a conversation. Also, if you have trouble coming up with questions for reviewers on the spot, extra time to consider can be helpful.

On the phone:

- *Pros:* Most of the benefits of in-person feedback, and you get a modicum of privacy to process.
- *Cons:* All of the cons of in-person feedback, and you don't get the benefit of seeing the other person's expression or body language.

In writing:

- *Pros:* You have all the time you need to process the review and your responses to it. You can carefully consider your responses and questions so that they target exactly what you want to learn.
- *Cons:* You have to infer tone and subtle meaning from your reviewers' words alone, which can sometimes make the feedback feel more critical. Also, you can't ask for more information or explanations in real time.

If you provided each of your reviewers with a questionnaire, you may receive at least part of your feedback in written form. However, it may also be helpful for you to plan a phone or in-person session to explore key concepts in greater depth and engage in conversation about some of the points that emerged in the critique.

Whether you are walking into a room or opening an e-mail, take a few moments to mentally prepare yourself for your feedback session, and to receive the actionable suggestions that come up. Open your heart to the possibility that the information you receive could be valuable, and even life-changing. Remember, you chose your beta readers because you trust them and value their opinions.

Below is a short meditation to assist you in preparing for feedback:

Pre-Feedback Meditation

Close your eyes, and take several deep breaths.
Imagine that your beta reader is sitting across from you. As you breathe, imagine a stream of white and golden light pouring down from above and enfolding both of you in its radiance.

As you watch, you can see the higher self of your beta reader standing behind him or her, with hands on your reader's shoulders. You can feel your higher self standing behind you as well, gently supporting you.

The eyes of your higher selves meet, and at the same time, you meet the eyes of your beta reader. As the golden and white light swirls around you and your higher selves, acknowledge that you are all in agreement about what will emerge from your upcoming conversation, and that any feedback will be delivered in a way which supports the highest good of all involved.

Thank your reader and his/her higher self for helping you to walk your path. Thank your higher self for assisting you through this process. Feel the love and trust that surrounds you.

Now, open your eyes, and proceed into your feedback session.

If you are speaking in person or on the phone, ask your reviewer at the start of the conversation to be honest but loving. Say something like, "I really want to get the most out of your feedback—but, as I'm sure you can imagine, I might need to process some challenging emotions during our session, so please bear with me." If you can, give your reviewer a few tools to support you through these moments. (You could even do the above meditation together!)

You can also remind your reviewer to offer solutions as well as opinions, so that you can actually take action on what's been shared; that is, after all, the point of the review.

However you choose to lay the groundwork for your sessions, though, don't ask reviewers to "take it easy on you," because their reticence might cause them to hold back some real gems.

Finally, if you feel yourself getting defensive during a conversation, ask to take a break until you can process what is coming up. After the initial rush of emotion, you may discover that your reviewer is, in fact, being helpful.

Non-Constructive Criticism
aka, The Ones Who "Tell It Like It Is"

Hopefully, you have chosen your reviewers with enough care that you won't need to deal with any deliberately hurtful comments. However, at some point you may have to contend with unforeseen circumstances—one of which is the reviewer who decides to "tell it like it is."

Usually, when someone precedes a comment with "I just have to tell it like it is," they are making an excuse for a bald judgment, and informing you that you must now accept their opinion as truth.

This happened to a client of mine. Before coming to work with me, she was told by another editor, "I'm sorry, honey, but I have to tell it like it is. You're just not a writer."

I'll be honest: when I heard that, it really pissed me off.

Of course my client is a writer! She writes almost every day. Before I met her, she had already self-published two books, and had spent months diligently creating sample chapters and proposal content for her third. Is she the contemporary incarnation of Dickens or Shakespeare? Maybe not—but that's not her calling. She's an entrepreneur, she's great at her job, and she has a lot to say. What's more, what she's saying is *valuable*.

In my mind, that makes her a writer.

It just goes to show you that "like it is" is a heck of a lot more subjective than most people want to admit.

In that editor's mind, she was telling the truth—and, having qualified that "truth" with "I have to tell it like it is," she excused herself from responsibility for her hurtful words.

As you can imagine, that statement hit my client like a ton of bricks. It took weeks for her to recover from the shame and embarrassment that editor's words brought up. Fortunately, she was wise enough to seek out other sources of feedback—but what if she hadn't done so? What if she had stopped writing forever, because of one person's thoughtlessly-offered opinion?

If you ever find yourself at the receiving end of someone's "telling it like it is," remind yourself that opinion—even highly-educated opinion—doesn't equal fact. If you retain nothing else from this section, please remember this: *You are not required to believe anyone else's opinion of you or your work.* You are the only person whose good opinion you require to keep writing, creating, and sharing your ideas with the world.

I sincerely hope that you never have to deal with a reviewer who tears you down. But if you do, rest assured: there are plenty of other people who will not share that person's opinion, so please seek them out before you let your inner critic take the wheel.

I'm happy to say that, at the time of this writing, my client's book proposal is in the capable hands of a top agent in her genre, and is being shopped to publishers. Obviously, there are plenty of people out there who *do* believe that she is a writer—and, thankfully, she is still one of them.

FEEDBACK STEP #4
TAKE ACTION ON YOUR FEEDBACK

Now that you have received feedback on your book, processed your emotions, taken note of the actionable items, and discarded the unhelpful stuff, it is time to implement what you've learned.

Obviously, I can't offer detailed action steps, because I don't know what specific feedback you received. I can, however, give you some general steps to get the most out of your reviewers' efforts.

How to incorporate feedback:

- *Look at the whole book, not just the specific section where you received feedback.* For example, if someone suggested that you adjust the way you relate a story, you will want to look not just at the story in question, but at every story in your book. Chances are, if you have done something in one place, you've done it in others, because human brains like repetitive processes.

- *Ask for a second review.* If you feel strongly that your reviewer is on to something, ask him or her to look at the changes you've made. Ask specific questions like, "Does this change address the issues you found?" or, "Does this addition help you connect more to my story subject?"

- *Use your feedback as a "course curriculum."* If you are not sure how to implement a suggestion, find the resources you need to do so confidently. Not sure how to make a story more exciting? Buy a book on story arc. Want to freshen up the dialogue? Find a free video tutorial on creating character conversations. Not sure how to shorten and target your sentences? Read up on Hemingway-style editing. There is a wealth of information out there, so please, tap into it. The worst that can happen is that you will affirm what you already know!

Work through each piece of feedback methodically and thoroughly. When you are done, set your draft aside for a day or so, then read through it again from start to finish, asking both the questions from Chapter 5, Step #2 in and the questions posed by your reviewers. Note any areas that need extra smoothing now that you have changed the material around them, and when you are done reading, do one final round of targeted revisions.

HOW TO WORK WITH AN EDITOR

If you have chosen to hire an editor to assist you with your book, this is a great time to send over your manuscript.

However, before you commit to working with an editor, there are a few things you will want to ascertain:

- *Does this person understand my genre?* There are a lot of great editors out there, but not all editors work in all genres. If possible, find an editor who specializes in the exact type of book you have written.

- *Does this person understand my voice?* If your editor focuses on academic writing, and you are using conversational voice, there may be a style gap there.

- *Do I like and trust this person?* In order to get the most out of the editing process, you need to be comfortable. If you feel like you are being patronized, belittled, or disrespected in any way, find someone else to work with.

Many editors offer free consultations or even sample edits. Take advantage of this so you can "meet" your editor and get a sense of his or her personality and energy. Ask questions about your editor's process and background, and share any fears or reservations you have about working with a professional. Then, see how the editor's responses land with you. Chances are, you will know right away if this will be a productive working relationship.

Once you find an editor you want to work with, there are some additional items you may want to ask for before you dive in.

- *Referrals.* Nothing beats talking to someone who has been there, done that. Ask your editor for the contact information of any past clients who might be willing to share their experiences.

- *A sample edit.* Most editors are willing to do a sample edit of ten pages or so (or a single chapter) for a small fee, or even for free. This is a great way to determine if your styles are a match, and if you feel comfortable with the individual editor's process. This also gives you a chance to ask questions about why the editor makes certain corrections.

- *A manuscript review.* This is a more extensive process in which the editor reads your entire manuscript and offers both a general opinion of the book and detailed suggestions for improvements to content, flow, and structure. This is a great place to start if you know your content needs help, and you suspect that you may need to make major changes to your book before it is ready for polishing (aka, line editing). Top editors may charge $500-$1500 (or more) for this service—but it is a worthwhile investment if you are serious about getting your book in shape. Also, this step may save time and money later, when it comes time to do your in-depth edit, because you will already have addressed many of your book's issues on your own.

- *A contract and price estimate.* If you are purchasing editing services, you will want to know exactly what those services entail. For example, if you are requesting line edits, you will want to know how many rounds of revision you are entitled to, how much it will cost if you add new material, and when you can expect your edited manuscript to be delivered.

What To Do When You Can't Choose Your Editor

If you opt to follow a traditional publishing path, you will probably be assigned an editor within your publishing house. Hopefully, this person will be someone with whom you can have a fabulous relationship—but if you end up feeling challenged, use the steps I've outlined in this chapter to get the most out of your experience.

Remember, editors are just regular people with sometimes stressful jobs. Like you, we have good days and bad days, successful days and "meh" days. But, like you, we have the best interests of your book at heart. If you do your best to be receptive to feedback, ask for clarification where you need it, and hold your intention for your book at the forefront of your mind, you and your editor will get along just fine.

MOVING ON

Hooray! You've made it through the gauntlet, and come out the other side a little more resilient than you were before. Plus, your book is better and more complete than it has ever been.

Next, you will tackle the additional components of your book, like your introduction, afterword, appendices, and reference sections. Then, it will be time to move on to your third and final draft!

chapter 7

THE MISSING PIECES

Your Introduction, Afterword, and Other Key Sections

Perhaps you've been wondering, "When am I going to write my introduction?" or, "Do I need a references section?"

There is a reason I usually wait until a book is nearly finished before writing these pieces. That reason is *clarity*. Until you know exactly what is in your book, it is hard, if not impossible, to write an effective introduction. Also, until you know the exact contents of your book and the order in which your citations appear, it's silly to format and finalize your list of references.

Therefore, we wait until the content of your book is firmly in place before we approach these final items. If you included an introduction in your outline, and wrote it as part of your first draft, great—but you will want go through it again using the tools in this section, and make sure that it is still accurate and compelling.

So, without further ado, here are the additional elements you may need to create for your book, in order of appearance.

YOUR TITLE

"Wait, what? I thought I already had a title!"

Yes, you do, and it's a great one. But, if you recall, it is a *working title*, and has always been subject to adaptation.

Now that your book is nearly complete, it is time to revisit your title and make sure that it still captures the essence and message of your book.

If you need to make an adjustment to your title or subtitle, revisit the title creation exercises in Chapter 1, and continue refining until you have it right. If you need help, poll your friends and social media followers.

YOUR BACK COVER TEXT

Your back cover text will evolve out of your purpose statement, and should reflect not only a sense of excitement about your book's contents but the overall tone, energy, and voice of your book.

Here are my suggestions for writing effective back cover copy:

- *Make every word count.* Your back cover layout may only allow space for 150-250 words of copy, so be sure that every word packs a punch.

- *Use your book's full title.* Don't refer to it as "the book," or "this book," unless the title appears in the previous sentence. If space is an issue, use the main title but leave out the subtitle.

- *Use short paragraphs.* You want people browsing online or in a bookstore to be able to digest your back cover copy rapidly, and get the most out of a single glance.

- *Use bulleted lists.* This is an easy-to-read way to share the primary benefits or teaching points of the book.

- *Write directly to your reader.* Instead of "Readers will learn," write "You will learn." Use teaching voice.

- *Keep your author bio short and sweet.* Readers can learn more about you on your bio page in the back of the book, or on your web site.

- *Include short excerpts from your endorsements.* If you have received reviews or testimonials for your book, add one or two on the back cover—and if you get a really great one from a recognizable name, add it to the front cover.

All in all, the purpose of your back cover is to entice people to buy your book, so don't be afraid to apply a heavy dose of marketing lingo and *braggadocio!*

YOUR COPYRIGHT PAGE

If you are self-publishing your book, you will need to include a standard copyright page with your manuscript. You can find generalized templates online from a number of sources. (At the time of this printing, there is a great example posted on TheBookDesigner. com.*) Or, simply modify the text from another book in your genre.

The most important components of the copyright page are:

Your name
© [Year of publication]. All Rights Reserved.

The second most important components are:

- Publisher's address, phone, e-mail, and other pertinent contact information (in case someone wants to license a portion of the book for reprinting).
- ISBN number (the barcode used for book distribution): your printer or publisher should have instructions about how to purchase an ISBN number. Or, you can go to Bowker.com to learn more.

- Library of Congress Catalogue Number (LCCN) if you are registering for one. (This is a good idea if you want your book to be available for order by libraries.) Apply at www.loc.gov, however be aware that it may take several weeks for you to receive your number, and you will need to obtain it before publishing your book.

- Your website URL.

Any other elements—like disclaimer text, details of rights, and credits for your editors and designers—can appear at your discretion. However, I'd advise you to stay close to the established templates, not because you can't do it better, but because readers are used to seeing certain pieces of information in certain places, and it makes it easier for them to find what they're looking for if they don't have to scan a giant block of text.

If you are publishing with a hybrid or traditional publisher, chances are the copyright page will be created for you, so you can skip this step.

YOUR DEDICATION

This is an optional piece, and pretty self-explanatory. It should be short—no more than a few sentences, a paragraph at most—and offer thanks or appreciation to one particular party.

Don't confuse the dedication with the acknowledgments. Those come later, and will give you plenty of space to thank everyone from your editor to your cat for the help they offered on this book project.

YOUR INTRODUCTION

Aside from your back cover copy, your introduction may well be the most important component of your entire book.

Many readers skim the introduction in the bookstore to determine whether they will buy the book. If your voice and subject matter doesn't hook them in those first few pages, they will put your book back on the shelf.

Also, if you are selling online, the introduction is usually the portion of the book showcased in the "free sample." If your introduction is weak, your book sales probably will be, too.

First and foremost, the introduction is where you should answer your readers' most burning question:

- Why should I buy this book?

You can convince them by answering these equally burning questions in your introduction:

- What is this book really about?
- What can I expect to learn from this book?
- What problem will this book help me solve?

You might also want to share:

- Why you chose to write this book (and any brief story elements that support that discussion).
- Why you are qualified to write this book.
- Any concepts with which you would like your readers to be familiar before diving into the book. (For example, if your book is about Transcendental Meditation, you might want to offer a brief description of TM and its merits in your introduction.)

Finally, pay close attention to the following:

- *Voice.* Your voice in the introduction should be strong and compelling, just like in the rest of your book

- *Language.* Remember, you are selling readers on your book in the introduction, so forego wishy-washy writing in all its forms. (More on this in Chapter 8.)

- *Length.* In most cases, shorter is better. There is no need to repeat information that readers can find in the body of your book.

YOUR AFTERWORD

Many writers won't need or want to include an afterword. However, here are some reasons why an afterword might be a smart addition to your book.

- You have additional instructions or takeaways for your readers which didn't fit seamlessly into your final chapter.

- You want to tell the story of how the book came into being (and didn't already do so in your introduction).

- You want to write a personal message to your readers to thank them for buying your book, express your wishes for their growth, or offer additional instructions.

- You want to ask readers to take additional action (like share a review of your book, or follow you on social media).

When writing your afterword, be sure to stay consistent with your tone, language, and message.

YOUR ACKNOWLEDGMENTS

Again, this is pretty self-explanatory. This section, placed at the rear of the book after your afterword (or after your final chapter), is where you will thank everyone who had a hand in helping you create your book.

Here are some people not to forget:

- Beta readers.
- Agents, editors, and publishers (if applicable).
- Mentors and teachers.
- Family and friends.
- The artist whose song inspired you.
- Your cat, who sits on your keyboard while you type.

Like all of your supplemental material, you will want to keep this short and sweet—ideally, no more than a page or two.

YOUR BIBLIOGRAPHY (AKA, REFERENCES)

Hopefully, if you've used copyrighted materials in your text—like song lyrics, fragments of famous speeches, or excerpts from other authors' books—you've kept notes on exactly where you found them, so that you can create a bibliography. Bonus points if you've added superscript numbers in your text where these excerpts appear (like this: (2)) or noted page numbers so you don't have to do the tedious work of finding them all again!

I know; the term "bibliography" is a bit outdated. Many of the references you cite may not be books at all, but videos, web pages, e-books, or audio recordings.

With this in mind, some authors choose to title their bibliographies "Notes" or "References" instead—but whatever you call this section, be sure to cite all instances of copyrighted material correctly to avoid copyright infringement.

The purpose of a citation is to ensure that readers can easily and quickly find whatever material you are referencing. Therefore, if you are quoting a paragraph from a book, you will not only need to know the book's title and author, but also the publisher, year of publication, and the page number from which the quote was sourced.

My favorite place to find citation guidelines is my trusty copy of *The Chicago Manual of Style* (see Resources Section).

(Notice how I did that? That's one way to direct readers to your bibliography!)

While there are too many different variations to cover here, I will share a few common citation formats to get you started.

Books

Author name [last, first], *Book title in italics.* (City and state where publisher is located: publisher name, year of publication), page.

Here's an example using my own information:

Haynes, Bryna René, *The Art of Inspiration: An Editor's Guide to Writing Powerful, Effective Inspirational and Personal Development Books* (Lakeville, MA: Inspired Living Publishing, 2016), p. 32.

There are numerous variations for books with multiple authors, books that are part of a series, reprint editions, etc. If your reference doesn't fit the standard criteria, look up how best to format your citation.

Articles

Author name [last, first], "Article title in quotations," *publication name in italics*, vol. number, page.

Here's an example from one of the contributors to this book.

Clark, Laura, "Let Your Intuition Be Your Sacred Self-Care Guide." *Aspire Magazine*, June/July 2016, p. 45.

Scientific Studies

If published in a journal, scientific studies are quoted in much the same way as other articles. If there are more than four study authors, use the citation, "et al." after the names of the primary authors. You can also include the DOI (Digital Object Identifier) number if available.

Author name(s) [last, first], "Article title in quotations," *publication name in italics*, issue or vol. number (or date), page, DOI number.

Here's an example I pulled from PubMed.

McMahon, D.M., "Living Well In Light of Science." Annals of the New York Academy of Science, 2016, May 10. DOI: 10.1111/nyas.13064.

Informal Online Publications

If you are citing material from a blog, online course, or other informal publication, provide whatever information you can, as well as a link back to the source. (It is understood that web links are subject to change.)

Author name (last, first), "Article Title in Quotations."
Website name in italics, date of publication, URL.

Here's an example from my blog.

Haynes, Bryna René. "4 BIG Reasons Why You Need an
Editor." *The Heart of Writing Blog*, April 8, 2016.
http://theheartofwriting.com/blog/2016/4/4/3-big-
reasons-why-you-need-an-editor.

Don't Be Fooled

Many authors make the mistake of pulling quotes directly from
internet quote sites, social media memes, or third party blog articles.
If you have sourced your quotes this way, you will need to do some
digging to find out where they really came from, and how to cite them
properly.

I've seen quotes from Marianne Williamson attributed to Nelson
Mandela, and quotes from modern fiction authors attributed to Ben
Franklin or Abraham Lincoln.

If you incorrectly attribute quotes because you didn't bother to
research, your credibility will take a big hit with discerning readers.
My advice is: if you can't find a credible, detailed source for a quote,
choose another quote.

Other Information Sources

Most formatting guides agree that you do have some latitude with
regard to how you format your citation, as long as all of your citations
contain the relevant information, and are consistent within your own
work. Again, it's all about making it easy for your readers to access the
information.

If you have only a few citations in your book (as in, not enough to fill one page), you can include them in footnotes, like I've done throughout this book. You can also include them directly in the text, like so:

> In her introduction to *The Art of Inspiration: An Editor's Guide to Writing Powerful, Effective Inspirational and Personal Development Books* (Inspired Living Publishing, 2016, p. 3), Bryna René Haynes writes ...

YOUR RESOURCES SECTION

You may choose to create a "Resources" section if you want to provide additional references or avenues of research for your readers.

For example, the Resources section in this book includes my top picks for writers' education and reference. This allows me to provide you with detailed, useful information without having to cram it all into the pages of this book.

The books, articles, and other materials in your Resources section should be cited in the same way as the references in your book's text. The only difference here is that you will leave out page numbers for books, since you are recommending the works in their entirety.

YOUR BIOGRAPHY

Your biography, or "About the Author" page, is typically the last section of your book (excepting the sales page, if you are using one). Here, you will share your credentials, list the titles of other works you have authored, and tell your readers a bit about yourself.

Your bio should be written in the third person, and structured something like this: (PS: this bio is completely fictional.)

Your name and what you do:

Suzy Somers is an accomplished medium, certified Life Coach, best-selling author, and frequent contributor to *Psychic Times* Magazine. Her first book, *Conversations With Ghosts*, was published in 2013 by GhostWriter Press, and received three book awards, including the prestigious [award name].

What you have accomplished:

Through her live events, one-on-one private sessions, and small-group tele-seminars, Suzy has helped thousands of people connect with loved ones who have transitioned to Heaven. The messages of love, hope, and purpose which she brings through the Veil have healed wounds, opened new doors of understanding, and radically transformed lives.

Your educational background (if applicable):

Suzy holds a Master's degree in Psychology from the University of Oregon, and a Bachelor's degree in Biology from the same institution. She received her Life Coaching certification through the World Coach Institute in 2005.

A bit of personal information:

Although she's still a West Coast girl at heart, today Suzy lives in Portland, Maine, with her husband and their daughter Julia. When she's not writing, she loves to play Frisbee with her rambunctious dogs, knit sweaters, and take long walks in the rain.

How to connect

Learn more about Suzy at www.SuzyMedium.com.

Additional Information

Include any additional information you like in your bio, but try to keep it under one page in length.

If you have written more than two books before this one, you can include an "Additional Works By [Your Name]" or "More Books By [Your Name]" page. This can be placed at the front of your book before the dedication, or at the end of the book after your bio. For this, you only need your book titles; it will look like this:

More Books by Suzy Somers

Conversations with Ghosts
Through the Veil

If you have only one other title credit, you can include it in your bio, and perhaps on your sales page.

YOUR SALES PAGE

If you offer services, classes, or products that will complement the information you have provided in your book, feel free to include a sales page at the end of your book, after your bio page.

This page usually includes images of your product and a brief description or testimonial, as well as links to your web page, social media, or online retailers where readers can find your offerings.

You can also create a sales page for another book, which might read something like,

> If you liked this book, be sure to check out Suzy's
> first book, *Conversations with Ghosts*, winner of three
> prestigious awards!

MOVING ON

Phew! You have filled in all the missing pieces of your book. Do your happy dance!

(In case you haven't noticed, I do a lot of happy-dancing.)

In your hands, you have something that could actually pass for a finished manuscript!

Well, almost. There is one final process to undertake before you are ready to give your book its wings, and that is your *self-edit*.

chapter 8

TAKING IT TO THE NEXT LEVEL

Self-Editing Basics and Refinement Techniques

Now that you've incorporated your feedback, compiled all of your book elements, and finalized your title, it is time to put your thinking cap on and dive into your self-editing process.

Are you ready?

For many writers, this can be a scary time. To take each sentence you have written, evaluate it, dissect it, and put it back together can feel a lot like major surgery: painful, vulnerable, and uncertain.

However, your self-editing process doesn't have to be devastating. In fact, it can be just as fun, creative, and educational as the rest of your writing process, if you have the right tools and mindset.

So, where do you begin?

I like to start with the big stuff—like sentences and paragraphs—and work my way inward to the minutiae, like punctuation.

Now, please keep in mind that, due to the nature of this book, I cannot possibly offer all the tools you will require for your self-edit in this single chapter. However, I hope to give you enough information to get you started on the path, and identify where you need additional support. In the Resources section, you will find a list of helpful books and references to deepen your understanding and refine your self-editing practice.

But before you dig in, I want to talk to you about *voice*.

SPEAKING VOICE VS. WRITING VOICE

"But what about my *voice*?"

If I had a nickel for each time I've heard this from a writer, I'd be living large in Monaco right now.

I think that this outcry—usually offered in resistance to editing of one sort or another—stems from two separate causes. One is insecurity, and a fear of being made "wrong." The other is a fundamental misunderstanding of what "voice" really means.

> *Your writing voice is the energy of your energy, purpose, vision, and personality, as transmitted through your words.*

When a writer has a strong voice, it often feels like s/he is speaking in your ear as you read. You can almost imagine that the writer is there with you, guiding you, teaching you what you need to know.

However, you may have noticed that, although the writer is "speaking" in your ear, that speech is not as casual as a normal conversation. It is more akin to oration. The inflection and lyrical quality of the writer's speech are obvious, but there are no "ums" and "ahs," no run-on sentences that trail off suddenly or shift direction in mid-thought, and no tangents or interjections.

In other words, a writer's "writing voice" is different than his or her "speaking voice"—but that doesn't make it any less authentic.

Most people write the way they speak. Spoken words are the most natural and automatic way for most of us to communicate, so we tend to default to that pattern, even when we're not actually speaking out loud. More, since our spoken words are our greatest tools for communication (and therefore relationship), we tend to associate our speech patterns with our identities.

When you look at it that way, it's no wonder that so many writers believe that if their writing doesn't mirror their speech exactly, their voice has been lost!

However "true" that belief may feel right now, though, you *must* release it if you want to write effectively.

Why?

When speaking conversationally (as opposed to orating), we are communicating off-the-cuff. That means that we draw heavily on our personal Top 1,000 words, and add many more descriptive words than necessary to make our point. As speech is fluid, and happens rapidly, these extra words aren't an issue. Plus, if someone doesn't understand what we're trying to say, we can always backtrack and throw more words at the problem.

Also, conversation is *erratic*. It moves like the wind, eddying here and there, picking up ideas and dropping them again. There are tangents, interjections, and reiterations. By the time you get to the point of a story, you may have touched on thirteen other topics. This works in conversation because conversation is dynamic, but it is a truly ineffective way to communicate on the page.

When writing, you only have *one chance* to make yourself understood by your readers. This means that you need to choose your words more carefully, and phrase your arguments more succinctly, than you would in conversation. This doesn't mean that your writing can't be *conversational*—but you need to acknowledge that it is a one-sided conversation, with readers unable to ask the questions they would normally pose in a dialogue.

The bad news is, if you write the way you speak, you will almost certainly need to take a metaphorical scalpel to your writing in order to make your book as powerful and impactful as possible.

However, the good news is, as long as you keep your purpose and vision front-and-center during your process, your self-editing will actually *strengthen* your voice, because you will have deleted any verbal clutter which clouded your purpose, vision, and personality. A clear pathway to connection is your top priority.

As long as the words you choose are aligned with your purpose and vision, they will be received in your voice. Therefore, shifting a sentence to create greater clarity for readers, or replacing your overused descriptors with more evocative ones, will not undermine your voice at all. In fact, with practice the editing process will teach you to communicate more clearly on all levels, even in day-to-day conversation!

Even if you spend twenty minutes poring over your thesaurus in search of a word that matches your energy, *you are still choosing the word*. You are making the effort to encapsulate your thoughts in exactly the right arrangement of letters. That means it is still yours.

There are plenty of other reasons to trust that your individual voice will come through in your writing, even if you make substantial changes in your self-editing process. Certain elements of voice are innate, and will characterize your writing whether you are aware of them or not. These include dialect- or preference-influenced word choices (*everyone* vs. *everybody*, *okay* vs. *alright*, *bubbler* vs. *water fountain*), as well as your unique responses to certain "stimuli" in your writing. (For example, would you write "It offends me that ..." or "It really pisses me off that ...?")

No matter how much you refine your writing, it is still *yours*. Knowing this will make the self-editing process easier and more productive for you.

Now, off to the races! It's time for your (amazing and totally enlightening) self-edit!

THIRD DRAFT STEP #1
EXAMINE YOUR ARCHITECTURE

In *Death in the Afternoon*, Ernest Hemingway wrote, "Prose is architecture, not interior decoration."

In context, the master was referring to the tendency of fiction writers to include metaphor, description, or prettified verbiage where it isn't strictly necessary. However, I think this particular quote can be applied in a much broader scope, and across multiple styles of writing.

Hemingway, Ernest, *Death in the Afternoon*, (New York: Charles Scribner's Sons, 1932)

Remember when I taught you about "killing your darlings" in Chapter 5? Right about now is when they start dropping like flies.

The first stage of the self-editing process is your line edit. This is where you will examine—you guessed it—*every line of your book*, and ensure that every single sentence does one or more of the following:

- Supports your readers' understanding of your topic.

- Creates an emotional bond between readers and your story or subject matter.

- Moves your narrative or argument forward toward your conclusion.

You are writing a non-fiction, inspirational book intended to share your world-changing ideas with a wide range of readers. This means that your writing should be clean, clear, and accessible, and that your greatest focus should be on *what you are saying* rather than *how you are saying it*.

Now, don't get me wrong; I'm not a minimalist. I'm a great fan of beautiful writing, even when it gets a bit long-winded. I love to read lyrical, haunting prose, and certain passages will create an indelible imprint on my psyche for decades.

However, you are not writing a book of poetry or personal essays. You are writing an *inspirational* book—and in order to do its job, your book needs not only to be read, but *understood* on a deep level by your readers. You would never teach mathematics in Shakespearean meter, even if it sounded beautiful; your students would be too distracted to actually learn anything. Similarly, if you ask your readers to wade through a sea of pretty but ultimately unnecessary words to get to the point of your lesson, they will quickly lose interest.

Therefore, focus on *teaching*, not performing. The natural beauty of your prose will still shine through—but it will be the beauty of a clean, bright hall, devoid of clutter, with a clear path to the doorway at its end.

The Basics of Line Editing

When you are ready to tackle your line edit, begin once more at the beginning.

Starting with the introductory materials you created in Chapter 7, read your book one sentence at a time. Read slowly. Read out loud. Read like you're a clam digger looking for those telltale bubbles in the sand.

In other words, stop looking at your book as a whole building, and look instead at every brick in its walls.

For every paragraph and sentence you read, ask yourself the following questions:

1. Does this sentence clearly and succinctly convey my desired meaning and energy?

2. Does this sentence or paragraph add new information to the narrative, or simply repeat something I've said before?

3. Is this sentence a fragment? If so, do I need to correct it?

4. Are my descriptive words targeted and evocative?

5. Have I used jargon or "genre-speak"? If so, have I defined all terms clearly in the text?

6. Have I used cliché descriptions or metaphors?

7. Have I used passive voice or excessive participles? If so, can I replace them without altering the meaning of the sentence?

(Don't worry, I'll give you the tools to answer these questions in the next section of this chapter!)

Line Edit Step #1: Meaning and Energy

As a rule, every one of your sentences should be concise; that is, they should express your desired meaning in as few words as possible. Note, as well, that "concise" doesn't always translate to "short"—but while it is a good idea to vary the length of your sentences in order to keep readers engaged, don't leave extraneous words lying around for the sole purpose of padding your prose.

Here are some examples of how "tightening up" your sentence construction can enhance your writing.

> *Wordy:* There are some people who just seem to have a natural gift when it comes to writing.
>
> *Tight:* Some people are natural writers.

> *Wordy:* I don't think many people fully understand the power that gratitude and thankfulness can have in their everyday lives.
>
> *Tight:* Most people don't understand the impact gratitude can have in their daily lives.

Notice how much easier it is to discern the meaning of the two more concise sentences. Also, the directness of the statements helps them feel "firmer."

How did I firm up those two sentences? I got rid of "filler" words.

Fillers are extra words that don't appreciably enhance the meaning of the sentence. In the first example, *there are, just, seem to,* and *when it comes to* are all fillers. Remove them, and the sentence becomes clearer.

In the second example, we see what I like to call an "Excuse Me" clause. As in, "Excuse me for having an opinion, but ..."

Since you are the author of the book, as well as the narrator, it is implied that every word in your book, (unless it is plainly quoted from another source), is your opinion.

Constant reminders like, "This is just my opinion," or, "It is my assertion that," make it seem like you are expecting an argument, or that you don't actually have any facts to support your assertions. Therefore, avoid Excuse Me clauses like *I believe, I think,* and *in my opinion,* unless you are a.) refuting something that is considered common knowledge, b.) making a statement you can't back up with fact or experience, or c.) expressing a matter of personal taste that isn't relevant to your readers' results (i.e., "In my opinion, maples are the most beautiful trees.")

Line Edit Step #2: New Information

I know that, for some of us, high school was a long time ago—but do you remember writing essays in English or History class?

At this remove, I can't recall a single word I wrote—but I *do* remember the cheating strategy I learned from a fellow student:

"Just write the same thing over and over, in different ways," he told me. "If you do it right, they'll never notice that you're not saying anything new!"

Sage advice, to be sure—and it worked! Most of the time, my teachers thought my writing was brilliant, and I was able to coast for three pages on a mere handful of original thoughts.

A+! *Bravissimo!*

Many of us still write that way, although our motives are vastly different. We're not looking for a cop-out; in fact, we want so badly to convey all the facets of our brilliant idea that we repeat ourselves over and over, trying to examine our topic from every possible angle.

However, rather than the intended effect of creating an unshakable connection with readers, this approach often backfires, and results in a lot of material that actually says very little.

It is absolutely necessary and desirable to review or reiterate key points in your narrative. (See Chapter 5, Step #3), but busy readers have neither time nor energy to follow a tangled or unnecessarily lengthy explanation, especially one that doesn't ultimately lead them to a new understanding.

Therefore, be sure that every paragraph offers some new piece of information, elaborates on or clarifies a previous assertion, or creates a transition from one idea to the next. If your paragraph doesn't do at least one of those things, revise it (or delete it altogether).

Line Edit Step #3: Sentence Fragments

Some sentences are chock full of unnecessary words. Others, however, may be missing *necessary* words.

I'm not going to include a full lesson on sentence structure here, but if you have questions, or if any of the terms I use in this section aren't familiar, please do check the Resources section for a list of helpful books.

Fragments are sentences which lack a subject (noun), an action word (verb), or both. For example:

- Leaving just when we were starting to like her. (No clear subject.)
- A book full of deep thoughts and insights. (No main verb.)
- From dawn until dusk. (No subject or verb.)
- Start next Monday. (No clear subject.)

Fragments can be tricky because they often show up in our habitual speech patterns, like this:

- "She totally pulled a fast one. You know what I mean. Leaving just when we were starting to like her."
- "Yes, you're hired. Start next Monday."
- "I worked like a dog, man. From dawn until dusk."

Unless you are writing actual dialogue, however, try to correct sentence fragments whenever possible. As you can see, adding the appropriate subject and verb form, or attaching the fragment to an independent clause (aka, a complete sentence) will solve the problem.

- *She left* just as we were starting to like her. (Or, *She pulled a fast one*, leaving just when we were starting to like her.)
- *It was* a book full of deep thoughts and insights.
- Yes, you're hired. *You can* start next Monday.
- *I worked like a dog*, from dawn until dusk.

Sentence fragments can also be formed by isolated *dependent clauses*. Dependent clauses are phrases which cannot stand alone outside of the context of the surrounding text, and which usually include a subordinating conjunction—a word like *because, by, before, after, although, where, when, while, unless, since, until*, or *if*, or a phrase like *as soon as, as much as, even though, so that*, or *now that*.

Often, dependent clause fragments are formed when we put a period where a comma should be.

- Because I couldn't make a choice.
- After I get my degree.
- While browsing the shoe department.

In order to correct the fragment, complete the thought or action within the sentence.

- *I stood there for hours*, because I couldn't make a choice.
- After I get my degree, *I'll go on my dream vacation.*
- While browsing the shoe department, *I broke my heel.*

It will be easier to spot dependent clauses now that you know what to look for. However, when sentences get longer and more complex, fragments like to hide in the mix.

If you aren't whether your sentence is actually a sentence (or just a dependent clause masquerading as one), pull it out of context. If it leaves you hanging—meaning, it leaves you with an unanswered question—it's probably a fragment.

- Because I couldn't make a choice ... (What occurred?)
- After I get my degree ... (Then what?)
- While browsing the shoe department ... (What happened?)

Fragments in modern writing

Although fragments are generally considered undesirable, there are a few ways in which modern writers use them deliberately.

One is the *list format*. Rather than use traditional punctuation with colons and semicolons, some writers opt to create a list using fragments. This has the effect of creating short, "punchy" sentences which convey strong emotion.

- She called me all the time. At noon. At bedtime. In the middle of the night. The calls never stopped.
- I wanted to believe that everything was okay. That life was just as it had always been. That all the hell I'd been through had washed off me like dust in a rainstorm.

Notice that each list begins with an independent clause that sets the tone for the list, and that each fragment a.) follows the same format and b.) begins with the same subordinate conjunction.

Another way to use fragments is to *ask and answer a question.*

- Why? Because I said so!
- Don't believe you have a problem? Think again.

You will probably recognize this format; it's common in advertising. I've also used it occasionally in this book. If you choose to write fragments in this way, be sure that they a.) fit the tone of the rest of the material, and b.) firmly answer the question which was asked, without incorporating extra information (save that for the next sentence).

Line Edit Step #4: Descriptive Words

Some of the most powerful tools in your writing toolbox are descriptive words. And, like all powerful tools, they are also among the easiest to misuse.

Why? Because most of the time, we choose descriptive words out of habit, rather than by their relevance to the material at hand.

In order to understand why we do this, we need to understand how we habitually use language.

The *Oxford English Dictionary*—considered to be the most complete chronicle of the English Language—contains over 170,000 words. (The unabridged version contains over half a million words!) However, almost no one uses more than a few thousand words on a regular basis. Most people have a "comfort-zone" vocabulary of about 20,000 words, with a larger, "passive" database of about 40,000 words. Shakespeare, the recognized master of wordplay, used about 70,000 different words in his plays—an immense number, to be sure, but still less than twenty percent of the words available to us today.

Seems like that would be enough to work with, right? But here's the thing: according to *The Reading Teachers' Book of Lists**, the first twenty-five words of our active vocabulary are used in 33 percent of our everyday writing, and the first 1,000 words are used in 89 percent of our everyday writing!

* Fry, E.B., Ph.D. & Kress, J.E., Ed.D. (2006). *The Reading Teacher's Book of Lists, 5th Edition.* San Francisco, CA: Jossey Bass.

I call these habitual words your *Top 1,000*. To make your writing as effective as possible, you will need to learn to think past them.

Your Top 1,000

Many of our Top 1,000 are simply common words like he, she, it, table, and car. They are words for the things, people, and places in our lives: in other words, nouns and pronouns. Other words in our Top 1,000 are verbs like type, drive, run, do, and have. However, many more of our Top 1,000 are dedicated to the words we use to describe these nouns and verbs. These are adjectives and adverbs—which, for our purposes today, will fall under the single category of descriptive words.

Ask any editor about how and where writers can improve their word choices, and s/he will probably answer: adjectives and adverbs!

Why? Because in many cases, these descriptive words are unnecessary and ineffective. And, as we learned in the section on meaning and energy, extra words dilute your message, and distract your readers.

How many times have you read a passage that described something as *beautiful, amazing,* or *incredible*? These are words commonly found in writers' Top 1,000, and their place at the top of our personal lists is reinforced by the fact that we see them every day in a variety of contexts. The trouble is not that these words are no longer functional, but that their overuse has made them ambiguous. What is beautiful to you may not be beautiful to me, and vice versa. ("And what," asks the cynic, "is beauty, anyway?")

Descriptive words with a wide range of possible meanings leave a writer's message open to interpretation—and, when you are writing with a purpose, this is the last thing you want.

If you type "overused descriptive words" into your online search engine, you will come up with hundreds of entries. It is worth it to spend some time perusing these lists, because some of them might surprise you. In the meantime, however ...

Here is a short (and by no means comprehensive) list of overused descriptive words that I encounter in my editing work every day.

1. Beautiful
2. Amazing
3. Incredible
4. Perfect
5. Gorgeous
6. Big
7. Little
8. Good
9. Bad
10. Quickly
11. Adorable
12. Interesting
13. Important
14. Best
15. Great
16. Very
17. Really
18. Totally
19. Huge
20. Wonderful

How do you know if a word is overused? Pay attention to what happens in your mind as you read it. You will probably notice that it conjures only vague images or feelings, as opposed to a specific vision.

The key to overcoming your dependence on overused descriptors isn't to weed them from your vocabulary entirely, but to recognize when they really are the best words for the task at hand, and when they appear by default.

Taking the time to examine and replace your overused descriptors will make your writing more powerful, concise, and interesting. It will also expand your everyday vocabulary, which certainly won't hurt your writing!

Here are five ways to improve your descriptive word usage and make your writing more powerful.

1. *Delete or pare down the descriptors.* Mark Twain wrote, "If you catch an adjective, kill it." The following are three ways to minimize your descriptive word usage and power up your prose.

Replace the word you are describing. If you find a long tail of two or more descriptive words, ask yourself if there is a way to replace the noun or verb instead. This is one of the simplest ways to make your writing more powerful.

- Is that "very big ship" really a ship—or is it a yacht, or a tanker, or an aircraft carrier?
- Did he "quickly run"—or did he dash, sprint, jog, or lope?
- Did that event "feel really bad"—or was it devastating, disruptive, or merely irritating?

Choose only one descriptor. There are places where descriptors are necessary, and even desirable. However, rather than leaving a long tail of mediocre words, choose only one powerful word to do the job.

- *Long:* He was an intelligent, resourceful, dedicated employee.
- *Short:* He was a top-notch employee.
- *Long:* The enormous mountain dominated the far horizon.
- *Short:* The mountain dominated the horizon.

Look for redundancies. Certain nouns and verbs imply certain qualities. For example, have you ever seen an ugly sunset? Seen someone dash slowly? Met a weak superhero? Probably not. Therefore, phrases like "beautiful sunset," "quickly running," or "powerful superhero" are redundant.

2. **Don't add unnecessary emphasis.** Adverbs like very, totally, definitely, truly, and extremely can call attention to verbs and adjectives, but use them sparingly. If you find yourself adding very every time you want to emphasize something, try strengthening your main word instead.

3. *Break up repetition.* Consult your thesaurus, and gather as many synonyms as you can find for the words you tend to use every day. Then, use your word processor's search function to highlight your go-to descriptive words, and examine each word in context. Is this thing you're writing about really "amazing?" Or is there another word that describes it more exactly?

4. *Choose where to emphasize.* The more description you throw at a subject, the more important it will seem to readers. This applies across the board, but especially in your stories, because your descriptors are powerful emotional triggers. For example, if you had a revelation about your relationship to the world while standing with your feet in the ocean, don't spend half a page describing the sunset. Instead, focus on the sensation of the waves lapping at your legs, and how you realized that the sand under your toes could have been brought here from halfway across the world.

5. *Check your alignment.* Do your descriptive words support the energy and vision of your purpose, and propel your readers toward the answers promised by your title? For example, if your aim is to show readers that people are inherently good, don't overuse words like *malice, betrayal,* and *mistrust.* As mentioned in the previous step, readers will focus their attention where your description is most concentrated—so make sure that your most powerful passages convey your purpose and mission, not the opposite.

Self-inquiry through adjectives?

It sounds counterintuitive, but a good way to know if you are on the right track with your descriptive writing is that it will feel *uncomfortable.*

Definitive statements which leave no room for interpretation can be scary to write. If you struggle in your day-to-day life to speak your truth or make yourself heard, you may also find yourself filling paragraphs with vague descriptors, hoping that readers will get the point without you actually having to come out and *say it*.

However, in a book designed to teach others and establish you as an expert in your field, this is tantamount to self-sabotage. Too many unclear descriptors can sap the power and conviction from your prose, and bog readers down in wishy-washy words that say very little.

If this sounds all-too-familiar, don't fret. Just being aware that you have this tendency can help you correct your weaker passages and bring greater clarity to your writing.

Line Edit Step #5: Clichés

Many of the descriptions we use every day are worn-out clichés. They are the first descriptions we think of when we're writing about certain events, and they are as comfortable and reassuring to us as our favorite pajamas.

Just as overused descriptors can feel vague and wimpy to our readers, so too do cliché expressions and descriptions feel boring and uninspired.

There are three kinds of clichés to watch for in your writing.

- *Cliché expressions* are those pieces of "folk wisdom" that crop up over and over. If you've heard it a hundred times before, it's a cliché.
  - As American as apple pie.
  - Every rose has its thorn.
  - Every cloud has a silver lining.
  - Read between the lines.
  - Money doesn't grow on trees.

- *Cliché descriptions* reiterate the things that everyone notices about particular people and situations, so they don't offer readers a new or interesting perspective.
  - Crashing waves and sparkling white sand (Is there something else you can notice about the beach?)
  - A gnarled oak tree. (Every oak tree is gnarled.)
  - A bustling city street. (Obviously. It's a city.)

- *Cliché reactions* are standard fare in storytelling. However, if you want readers to pay close attention to what your character is doing, find a new way to demonstrate it.
  - Hot tears spilling down my cheeks.
  - Teeth clenched in anger.
  - Cheeks growing red in embarrassment.
  - Eyes narrowing in suspicion.

Obviously, cliché expressions, descriptions, and reactions are cliché for a reason: they're accurate. However, when your readers' attention really counts, try to find a new and inventive way to describe what is happening.

Line Edit Step #6: Jargon or Genre-Speak

Have you noticed that every field of study has its own language?

Profession-specific terminology, acronyms, and other jargon may make you sound important and in-the-know, but unless you are writing a book solely for people in your field of study, these terms can actually create a barrier between you and your readers. No one likes to feel like they are being excluded or talked down to.

If your narrative requires the use of professional jargon, be sure to clearly and conspicuously define each new term as it is introduced. That way, your book feels inclusive, as though you are letting your readers in on your professional secrets.

"Genre-speak" is a bit different than professional jargon, but can be just as divisive. As I've mentioned elsewhere in this book, it is a mistake to assume that everyone who reads your book will be familiar with your genre and influences.

Therefore, avoid statements that assume readers have had certain experiences or follow certain belief systems, unless you have made it clear with your title, subtitle, and back cover text that your book is intended for a very specific audience. (For example, if your subtitle includes the words "For Yoga Teachers," you can assume that your readers will be familiar with the fundamentals of yoga practice. Similarly, if your subtitle is "Practices for Christians ..." your readers will likely be familiar with the Bible.)

If your book's premise relies on your readers' understanding of foundational concepts such as past lives, the Law of Attraction, manifestation, thought as energy, or any other concepts which may not be standard fare for the average Jane Doe, be sure to explain your personal understanding of these fundamentals in your introduction or Chapter 1. This will not only educate your novice readers, but will also give "seasoned" readers a valuable glimpse into your personal viewpoint and approach.

Line Edit Step #7: Participles and Passive Voice

Active, decisive verb forms are vital to powerful writing. When you overuse participles and passive verb forms, it softens your message and makes it less memorable.

Participles

Verbs ending in "-ing" often don't come across strongly. Why? Because this construction (participle form) generally indicates that the action is *happening and continuing to happen*, so it is fluid.

If you find that most of your verbs end in "-ing," you can strengthen your message by using the *infinitive* form of the verb, as follows:

- My plan will help you with *writing* and *editing* your book.
- My plan will help you *write* and *edit* your book.

- While we were *driving*, we were *singing* and *taking* pictures.
- While we *drove*, we *sang* and *took* pictures.

- *Dancing* and *painting* are two of my favorite things to do.
- I love to dance and paint.

In many cases, "-ing" verbs are proceeded by some form of the verb "to be," so look for the words *am, are, is, was*, and *were*.

(Bonus: when you utilize a more direct form of the verb, that extra word can be cut!)

Passive voice

Passive verbs remove emphasis from the *doer* of the action, and place it on the *receiver* of the action. This can have the effect of absolving the subject from responsibility for the action.

Passive constructions have their place, of course, but when overused they can dilute the power of your message.

Here are some examples of passive and active construction.

- *Passive:* The ruling was overturned in the Senate.
- *Active:* The Senate overturned the ruling.
- *Passive:* My book was written while I was on vacation.
- *Active:* I wrote my book while on vacation.
- *Passive:* The wall was damaged during the night.
- *Active:* Last night, I kicked a hole in the wall.

How can you tell if a verb is passive? Like participles, passive verbs often integrate forms of the verb "to be."

Also, as I mentioned, passive constructions leave the "doer" out of the picture. "My book was written while I was on vacation"—but by whom? Me? Or did someone else write it while I was gone?

To avoid this kind of ambiguity, use direct verb forms.

Completing your line edit

Once you have examined, restructured, compressed, and de-clichéd every sentence in your draft, your line edit will be complete.

You probably have steam shooting out of your ears at this point (notice the cliché there?), but if you can stand it, it's a good idea to go through your manuscript one more time, reading each section aloud to ensure that your newly-upgraded sentences flow naturally.

Once you are satisfied with the state of your line edit, it will be time to move on to *proofreading*.

THIRD DRAFT STEP #2
PROOFREAD & FORMAT

This is the really technical work of editing. In this phase, you will verify that all of your punctuation, formatting, and stylistic choices are correct and consistent; that your piece is free of typos and spacing errors; and that all names, quotations, and excerpts are accurately spelled, formatted, and cited.

If you think this sounds a bit scary, you are not alone. But I promise, learning to proofread is not hard. It just takes a little bit of time, willingness, and the right resources.

When proofreading, I like to reference my "style sheet"—a checklist I've created over the years of common errors and formatting issues. This sheet gets updated for every editing project so that it includes each author's personal terminology, preferences, etc.

On the following pages, you will find a short list of items on my permanent style sheet, with explanations.

Remember, what I've provided here are only the bare basics of solid proofreading. Keep notes on your common mistakes so you can compile your own style sheet—and don't forget to check the Resources section for some great books on grammar, punctuation, and style.

A final note on publishing and proofreading:

- You should *always* proofread your document before submitting it to a publisher or agent.

- If you are self-publishing, you should proofread your document a second time, after your designer has copied your manuscript into the design layout. This will ensure that all italicized words, punctuation, formatting and other items have transferred correctly, and that no text was lost in the cut-and-paste process.

BRYNA'S STYLE SHEET

Names

- Check all names to be sure that they are capitalized and spelled properly.

Dates

- Be sure that dates are formatted in exactly the same way throughout the document. In articles, books, and e-books, this usually means like this: "December 12, 2011." Subscript abbreviations (December 3rd) are generally not used in these formats. Decade references can appear like this: the 1960s, the '60s, or the Sixties. However, only one format should be used throughout the text.

Numbers

- In general writing, most numbers under 100 should be written out in long form (ex: *she had ninety-nine balloons*), while numbers over 100 should appear in numerical form (ex: *he had 432 pages of citations*).
- Ages should always be written out (*ex: she turned fifty-two today*).
- Percentages should be written as "45 percent" except in scientific or academic texts, where the percent sign (%) can be used.

Quotations

- Be sure all quotes are properly attributed in the text and/or appendices.

Citations

- Make sure the punctuation, spacing, and overall format of your citations are consistent and accurate.

Spacing.

- The old rule of double-spacing after a period dates to the age of typewriters, and no longer applies. Make sure there is only one space after periods, commas, colons, semicolons, and all other punctuation.
- Also check the spacing between paragraphs, below headers and titles, above footers, and along the right-hand edge of the text (sometimes referred to as the "rag").

Punctuation

- Check to be sure that:
    - All sentences end with a period.
    - Commas appear when appropriate. (Decide ahead of time whether you will use Oxford commas—aka serial commas—or not, and apply formatting consistently throughout.
    - The first letter of the first word of every sentence is capitalized.
    - All quotes, excerpts, and dialogue have both opening and closing quotation marks, and punctuation appears appropriately inside and/or outside the quotation marks.
    - Periods and commas appear inside quotation marks, while colons and semicolons appear outside. Exclamation points and question marks appear either inside or outside, depending on how they relate to the quoted material.
    - All parenthetical statements have both opening and closing parentheses, and punctuation appears appropriately inside or outside the parenthetical statement.
    - Colons and semicolons are used appropriately.
    - Em-dashes (—) should not have spaces on either side.
    - Ellipses (…) should have spaces on either side. In most cases the first word of the sentence after the ellipsis is capitalized.

Commonly Mixed-Up Words

- There are many words which may be incorrect in context but will not show up as errors during a spell check. Here are a few mix-ups I see all the time.

    - you/your
    - your/you're
    - their/there/they're
    - quite/quiet
    - who's/whose
    - business/businesses
    - woman/women
    - its/it's
    - advise/advice
    - fell/feel
    - though/through
    - though/thought
    - arc/arch
    - affect/effect
    - founder/flounder
    - further/farther
    - accept/except

- I recommend using your search function to identify all instances of these commonly misused words so that you can check them individually—especially you/your and its/it's, because these are easy to skim over when you are reading.

VOICE AND THE EDITOR

"Okay," you say, "I think I've got this self-editing thing down pat. I even feel like my book is still in my voice! But what happens when I work with someone else, like an editor?"

One of the biggest complaints I hear from clients who have worked with other editors is, "S/he totally changed my voice!"

I won't say it doesn't happen; in fact, I've seen it many times. However, it is important to remain aware that, just like with your beta readers, an editor's feedback can prompt you to react defensively.

Here's my take on writing voice with an editor's input.

A good editor (by which I mean, the right editor for you) will work to identify vital elements of your voice and preserve them throughout the document. These elements may include personal preferences for phrasing, branded phrases for your business, and quirky word usages that don't detract from readers' comprehension. If you are working together in depth (for example, through the development stages of your book) s/he may even record phone sessions with you, in order to better study your communication style while clarifying specific points about your project.

However, a good editor will also ask you really hard questions, and will reposition or even cut any content that doesn't serve the finished product. S/he will also take out words that you tend to use over and over, change instances of passive voice, and remove those pesky "-ing" participles wherever appropriate. S/he will condense your run-on sentences, correct your punctuation, and move whole sentences and paragraphs around in order to allow your message to come through clearly.

So, how do you know when your voice has been compromised?

It's more of a feeling than anything else.

When you are done working with an editor, your piece should read like its own best possible self. Just as you would dress carefully, style your hair, and put on snazzy shoes to meet your next top client, so too will the editing process dress up your prose so that it can show its best face to your readers. This process of refining is not an assault on your voice, but rather an enhancement of it.

There is a line, however, between in-depth editing and rewriting. It's the difference between skillful makeup and plastic surgery.

Sometimes, an editor's rewrite can work in your favor: a new perspective can give your book a necessary boost, and address points you hadn't thought of. However, if you read something added or corrected by your editor, and think, "I would never say that," or if you feel like your editor is trying to leave her mark on your writing for egotistical or business purposes, speak up. Any editor worth her salt will be happy to explain her choices, correct her missteps, and work beside you to create a book you can be proud of.

MOVING ON

Wow. Holy cow. You have a finished manuscript in your hands! Happy dance, happy dance!

But now that your book is finished, what do you *do* with it?

Read on to discover your options, and get ready to get your book out there!

part 4

polish & refine

chapter 9

FROM YOUR DESK TO READERS' HANDS

Identify Your Ideal Publishing Option

Now that you've finished your manuscript, what should you do with it?

Well, first, do *another* happy dance. Maybe host a dance party. Tell the world that you have FINISHED YOUR BOOK!

Seriously. You've come through the "ring of fire," and done what the vast majority of would-be authors fail to do: you've joined the exclusive group of people who have *actually finished a book.*

How amazing is that?

Bask in your accomplishment for a good day or two. Feel the depth and breadth of your mighty feat.

Then, put that brilliant creative mind to work, and start thinking about how to get your book off your desk and into the world.

How should I publish?

There are loads of ways to get your work out there. Not all of them may be right for you at this time.

Publishing is an art and science all its own, and there are hundreds of books, courses, blogs, and conferences dedicated to helping writers choose the right path. As an editor, I deal mostly with the parts of the process that happen before a writer is published—and, while I have some knowledge to share, I also want to be honest and authentic: my expertise does not extend to the publication, marketing, and distribution of books.

However, since I don't want to leave you (and your amazing book) stranded in the middle of the forest without a guide, I will give you enough information here to help you choose a general direction, and find your way to the resources that will aid you most in your personal publishing journey.

So, let's begin at the beginning.

WHAT DOES IT MEAN TO PUBLISH A BOOK?

Publishing a book simply means that you have made it available, in some form, for the public to view. You can publish in your book in print, digitally, or in an audio book format.

When most people think of "publishing," they also think of printing. I won't lie: it's a pretty amazing feeling to hold your own book in your hands! However, since we live in a digital age, the physical process of printing is not necessary to publish your book; releasing your book as an e-book is still publishing it!

When you start to consider how to publish your book, ask yourself the following questions:

- What is my greatest dream for my book?
- How do I want my book to serve me? (As a resource for my clients, for my family and friends, as a compliment to my speaking platform, as a way for me to emerge as an expert in my field, etc.)
- Where do I want people to be able to find my book? (Online, in bookstores, etc.)
- What is my ideal timeline for publishing my book?
- What is my maximum budget?

All of the above factors will help you determine which publishing route is right for you.

Path #1: Self-Publishing

Self-publishing is exactly what it sounds like: a way for you to publish on your own.

For many writers, this is an ideal option. (You'll see why when you read the pros and cons.) However, be aware that doing it on your own is rarely as easy as sending in your manuscript and clicking "publish." For one, you will need to supervise everything from start to finish, and there may be a steep learning curve involved. Second, you will be solely responsible for the marketing of your book, so if you don't put forth the effort to let your audience know you have written a book, no one may ever know it's out there.

Here are my pros and cons for self-publishing.

Pros:

- *There are no qualifications to meet.* You don't need to be vetted by agents or editors to self-publish. As long as you can pay the fees, you can publish whatever you want.

- *You can do it on your own timeline.* Basically, as soon as you have your files ready, you can publish. No deadlines or wait times.

- *You have full control* over cover design, interior formatting, and the editing process. You won't be subject to anyone else's ideas about how your book should look.

- *You can publish under your own "imprint."* You don't need to use your printer's name on your book. In fact, you can create a "publishing house" with any name you choose. (Note: there may be some legal work involved in this. Talk it over with your accountant or attorney.)

- *You'll get larger royalties.* When you self-publish, you are responsible for the costs of printing and distribution (including fees to Amazon and other digital marketplace platforms)—but beyond that, all of the profit is yours.

Cons:

- *You won't get an advance.* Also, you will be responsible for all the costs of editing, printing, marketing, promotion, and distribution.

- *You have to do it all on your own.* You don't know what you don't know about publishing—but you will need to learn if you want your book to be top-notch.

- *You will definitely need to hire an editor.* Although this is changing in the current market, self-published books historically have a poor reputation. Why? Because at one time, most self-published books were unedited. No one wants to read a book full of typos and formatting mistakes. Even if you are super-talented in the grammar department, it is vital to have a professional pair of eyes on your work before you send it out into the world.

- *You will need to pay for design.* Although most self-publishing companies offer book design and cover design services at a moderate cost, their designs are often based on templates, and aren't always very attractive. (Ask your self-publishing company to see samples of their book covers and decide for yourself.) If you are competent with software like Photoshop or InDesign and want to try designing your own cover and interior layout, that's great (most self-publishers have guidelines you can follow for spine width and margins) but if not, you will want to hire a designer.

- *You will need to market your book.* Self-publishing companies may make your book available to order on

Amazon, Barnes & Noble, and in certain catalogues, but they won't let anyone know your book is there. And, since there are more than 250,000 titles published every year in the United States alone, you will need to do more than just wait for people to find you.

Hybrid Publishing

Hybrid publishing companies integrate some of the best practices of both self-publishers and traditional publishers. However, they are still fee-for-service companies—and since their services are often niche-based and specialized, they may be more expensive than straight-up self-publishers.

Pros:

- *You get all the benefits of self-publishing, and then some.* You still own your work and get substantial royalties, but have the benefit of publishing under the imprint of the hybrid publisher, and taking advantage of their connections for sales and distribution.

- *You get an expanded platform.* Most hybrid publishers have sales channels that reach beyond where straight-up self-publishers can go. Some have integrated marketing and launch programs designed to create greater visibility. However, this varies from company to company, so be sure to research your chosen publisher before moving forward. The best way to assess a company is to speak with authors who have published with them.

- *You may get higher quality.* With hybrid publishers, you are more likely to receive quality cover design and layout—but again, this isn't true across the board. Check the publisher's samples to be sure that they speak to you. If not, hire your own designer.

- *You get greater credibility.* Hybrid publishers are likely to have a vetting process because their reputation depends on publishing quality books.

Cons:

- *They can be expensive.* Because you are getting better service and distribution channels, expect to pay more.
- *They may have a vetting process,* based on their brand and quality standards. So even if you want to publish with a certain imprint, you are not guaranteed a spot on their roster.
- *You will still have to hire an editor.* Even if your book is accepted as-is, it is still wise to have an editor polish your work before publication. Some hybrid publishers may require this step as well.
- *You will still have to do most or all of the marketing yourself* (unless you purchase a marketing package from your publisher).

TRADITIONAL PUBLISHING

Pros:

- *You will get the prestige* of a big name behind your book.
- *You will get an in-house editor and design team.*
- *You will get the most extensive distribution channels in the industry.* Online, bookstores, specialty, stores, you name it: your publisher can get you in there.
- *You will have very little, if any, up-front cost.* You may even get an advance!

- *You will have an agent representing your work.* Most traditional publishers do not accept unsolicited manuscripts, so you will need an agent to submit your book to editors on your behalf. Agents manage a lot of the details that frustrate self-published and hybrid-published authors, including sales to foreign markets, media rights, and other elements.

Cons:

- *You will have a much longer timeline.* It may take a year or more from the time your book is accepted for it to land on bookstore shelves.

- *You will need to work through an agent.* Connecting with the right agent to represent your book takes time and energy. You will need to write query letters and a killer book proposal (which is an art unto itself). Also, once you land an agent, there is no guarantee that the agent will be able to sell your book to a publisher.

- *You will get much smaller royalties.* And, you will need to "pay back" your advance in book sales before you are paid another dime. Your agent will take around 15 percent of your royalties. (The flip side of this, of course, is that with better distribution, you will probably sell more books.)

- *You won't get to choose your editor or designer.* These decisions are made by your publishing house. You may have some input, but you won't have veto power.

- *You will still have to market your book.* Traditional publishers usually spend their marketing dollars on the authors they know can sell books. As a new author, you may be expected to hire your own publicist, as well as maintain your own website, social media pages, and other marketing channels.

HOW TO PROCEED

Once you have decided which avenue of publishing is right for you, it will be time to take the next steps toward releasing your book into the world.

As you research your chosen platform, your specific action steps will become clearer to you—but for now, here are some general next steps for publishing in each genre.

Self-Publishing:

- Establish your budget.
- Find and hire an editor.
- Find and hire a designer (or work with your self-publishing company's design team).
- Set your publication date and work your marketing mojo.

Hybrid Publishing

- Research your company's reputation, success stories, and pricing.
- Submit your manuscript for review (if necessary).
- Outline next steps with a company representative, including hiring an editor and/or designer, marketing your book, etc.

Traditional Publishing

- Identify agents in your genre.
- Craft a great query letter and start sending it to agents.
- Start working on your book proposal. (A good editor or book coach can help you with this if you're struggling.)

AND FINALLY ...

By sharing your wisdom and expertise with readers, you have done the world a great service.

Regardless of how many copies of your book you ultimately sell, or how many speaking gigs you land, I hope that you always remember the purpose and vision you started with, and how much of an inspiration you truly are to those whom your work has touched.

So go forth, writer, and *inspire*!

Blessings,

Bryna

PS: Don't forget to keep in touch! I can't wait to hear about what you're creating!

resources

BOOKS ON THE ART AND PRACTICE OF WRITING

These are a few of my favorite guides to writing. They range from spiritual to practical, but all have interesting tidbits.

Goldberg, Natalie, *Writing Down the Bones: Freeing the Writer Within* (Boulder, CO: Shambhala Publications, 1986)

Cameron, Julia, *The Artist's Way* (New York, NY: Jeremy P. Tarcher/Putnam, 1992-2002)

King, Stephen, *On Writing: A Memoir of the Craft.* (New York, NY: Pocket Books, 2000)

Zinsser, William, *On Writing Well* (New York: HarperCollins, 1976-2006)

DICTIONARIES & THESAURI

Westley, Miles, *The Bibliophile's Dictionary: 2,054 Masterful Words and Phrases.* (Cincinnati, OH: Writer's Digest Books, 2005)

Rodale, J.I., *The Synonym Finder.* (New York: Rodale Press, 1978)

Laird, Charlton; Agnes, Michel, et al., *Webster's New World/ Roget's A-Z Thesaurus.* (Cleveland, OH: Wiley Publishing, 1999

GRAMMAR, PUNCTUATION, AND EDITING
A short list of the references I use in my editing work.

The Chicago Manual of Style, 15th Edition (Chicago, IL: The University of Chicago Press, 2003)

Strunk, William Jr.; White, E.B., *The Elements of Style, 4th Edition.* (WLC Books, 2009)

Truss, Lynne, *Eats, Shoots, & Leaves: The Zero Tolerance Approach to Punctuation.* (New York: Penguin, 2003)

Merriam-Webster's Dictionary of English Usage (Springfield, MA: Merriam-Webster, 1994)

Levine, Alice, *The Copyeditor's Handbook.* (Los Angeles, CA: University of California Press, 2006)

DIALOGUE AND OTHER FICTION ELEMENTS

Chiarella, Tom, *Writing Dialogue: How To Create Memorable Voices and Fictional Conversations that Crackle with Wit, Tension, and Nuance.* (Cincinnati, OH: Story Press, 1998)

Noble, William, *Conflict, Action & Suspense.* (Cincinnati, OH: Writer's Digest Books, 1994)

Hood, Ann, *Creating Character Emotions: Writing Compelling, Fresh Approaches that Express Your Characters' True Feelings.* (Cincinnati, OH: Story Press, 1998)

PUBLISHING, BOOK MARKETS, AND OTHER

Larsen, Michael, *How to Write a Book Proposal, 4th Edition.* (Cincinnati, OH: Writer's Digest Books, 2011)

Writer's Market 2016 (Cincinnati, OH: Writer's Digest Books, 2016)

Crawford, Tad; Murray, Kay, *The Writer's Legal Guide: An Authors Guild Desk Reference, 4th Edition.* (New York, NY: Allworth Press, 2013)

Norwick, Kenneth P; Chasen, Jerry Simon, *The Rights of Authors, Artists, and other Creative People, Second Edition: A Basic Guide to the Legal Rights of Authors and Artists (ACLU Handbook).* (Carbondale, IL: Southern Illinois University Press, 1992)

OTHER RESOURCES

Here are a few people and businesses whose services you may find valuable. Keep in mind, these are my personal recommendations only; before working with any person or company, do your research to be sure they meet your needs and serve your vision.

Createspace
A self-publishing company that many of my clients have successfully used to publish and distribute their books.
www.Createspace.com

Inspired Living Publishing
Founded by Linda Joy, ILP focuses on bringing the messages of heart-centered women entrepreneurs to light. Linda's hybrid publishing model includes powerful marketing packages.
www.InspiredLivingPublishing.com

Lisa Tener, Book Coach
Lisa is my favorite resource for clients who are following a traditional publishing path. Her blog is also chock full of great interviews and information for writers in all genres.
www.LisaTener.com

acknowledgments

I couldn't have brought this book to life without the help of many inspiring individuals:

My husband, partner, and twin flame, Matthew, who stayed up late analyzing drafts and processes, and did more than his fair share of *everything* while I scrambled to pull the book together. Thanks for believing in me—and for the love notes you left in red pen on the final draft!

My daughter, Áine, who reminds me what is really important.

My wise and compassionate sister, Ana, for being the best sister a girl could ask for—and the best Auntie a Moonbeam could ever have.

My mama, Sue; my papa and stepmother, Bernie and Deryl; my more-than-just-in-laws, Ed and Jackie; Alessandro the Great, and my sister-from-another-mother, Lauren. Your steadiness and love make my life rich and my wild dreams possible.

My good friend (and now publisher) Linda Joy, whose unconditional support, generosity, and supercharged "divine downloads" have been a light in my life for the last six years.

Book coach Lisa Tener, my friend and role model, who offered both sage advice for my readers and loving encouragement for me.

The inspiring, dynamic writers who contributed their knowledge and experience to this process, and helped me answer all the right questions: Dr. Debra Reble, Peggy Nolan, Laura Clark, Mal Duane, and Karen Spaiches.

And, last but not least, my beloved clients, friends, and fellow writers—especially Boni Lonnsburry, whose words grace the cover of this book. Thank you for trusting me with your words, and allowing me a chance to nurture your world-changing visions. You are *my* inspiration.

contributors

The following people contributed their valuable time, energy, and experiences to this book. Their feedback helped me shape many of the lessons and processes I've created, and gave me further insight into the daily lives of inspired writers.

Lisa Tener, book coach, was awarded "Mentor/Coach of the Year" in 2014 by the Stevie Awards for Women in Business, She is an inspiring book writing and publishing coach, author, and speaker. Her clients have signed 5- and 6-figure book deals with HarperCollins, Simon and Schuster, Random House, Scribner's, HCI, Beyond Words, New World Library, Hay House, New Harbinger, Yale University Press, Johns Hopkins University Press, ABC-CLIO and other major publishers, as well as self published. Her *Bring Your Book to Life* Program won The Silver Stevie Award for Best New Service of the Year-Media in the American Business Awards 2012, and she was awarded The Gold Award for Marketer of the Year in Media. Learn more at www.LisaTener.com.

Dr. Debra Reble, international best-selling author of *Being Love: How Loving Ourselves Creates Ripples of Transformation in Our Relationships and The World*, and the award-winning *Soul-Hearted Partnership: The Ultimate Experience of Love, Passion, and Intimacy.* Consciously merging her practical tools as a psychologist with her intuitive and spiritual gifts, Debra empowers women to connect with their hearts and live authentically through her transformational Soul-Hearted Living™ program. Learn more at www.DebraReble.com.

Laura Clark, international best-selling coauthor of *Inspiration for a Woman's Soul: Cultivating Joy,* and *Inspiration for a Woman's Soul: Choosing Happiness,* is known as the Soul Wise Living Mentor. She works with overwhelmed professionals to stop listening to the negativity within them and get off the emotional roller coaster that delays action. Laura uses a unique blend of spiritual awakening tools to help her clients hear their own intuition consistently, understand it clearly, and act upon it courageously to lead inspired lives filled with joy and abundance. Discover more at www.SoulWiseLiving.com.

Peggy Nolan is the author of *Can't Die Mom*, the coauthor of four best-selling books (including *Inspiration for a Woman's Soul: Cultivating Joy* and *Inspiration for a Woman's Soul: Choosing Happiness),* and the creator of the popular podcast, *Let Go Move Forward.* She is passionate about leadership and personal growth. She teaches yoga, she's a third-level black prajioud in Muay Thai Kickboxing, and she's a breast cancer survivor who's been slaying doubt and vanquishing fear since 2004. She lives in Derry, NH with her husband, Richard. Connect with her at www.PeggyNolan.com.

Mal Duane is the award-winning author of *Alpha Chick: 5 Steps for Moving from Pain to Power* and a coauthor of the international best-selling *Inspiration for a Woman's Soul: Choosing Happiness.* as well as a contributor to MariaShriver. com, *Healthy Living, Huffington Post*, and *Aspire Magazine*. An inspirational speaker, life coach and highly successful real estate business owner, Mal is a champion for restoring women's self-worth. She helps women heal their broken hearts and reclaim their lives. Learn more at www.MalDuaneCoach.com

Karen Spaiches is a personal life coach who engages with women who feel lost and unsettled. She helps clients unleash long-forgotten dreams, to stop settling for the "good enough" and to take passionate action in creating their ideal life. She nurtures and empowers women to live their highest potential through creating powerful habits of self-love and self-acceptance. Karen's personal rediscovery journey set the stage for her signature program, "Dream Life Design." Learn more at www.KarenSpaiches.com.

about the author

"Word Alchemist" Bryna René Haynes is the President and founder of The Heart of Writing, the chief editor for Inspired Living Publishing, a published author, and an experienced freelance writer and editor. She loves helping authors break through their perceived limitations to tap into their authentic voices, show up fully on the page, and create books that embody and empower their visions and dreams.

Bryna's editing portfolio includes numerous successful non-fiction titles (including national and international best-sellers) and nationally-published articles, as well as Inspired Living Publishing's best-selling print anthology series. She continually collaborates with industry and media experts to create personally-tailored, print-ready book packages for her private clients.

A proud Rhode Islander (minus the accent), Bryna lives outside of Providence, RI with her gondolier husband, Matthew, and their daughter, Áine. When she's not writing, you can find her teaching yoga philosophy, exhibiting her landscape and travel photography, and singing silly songs with her Moonbeam.

Learn more about Bryna's current projects, editing and coaching services, and workshop offerings at www.TheHeartofWriting.com.

about the publisher

Founded in 2010 by Inspirational Catalyst Linda Joy, Inspired Living Publishing (ILP) is an international best-selling inspirational boutique publishing company dedicated to spreading a message of love, positivity, feminine wisdom, and self-empowerment to women of all ages, backgrounds, and life paths.

Through our highly successful anthology division, we have brought seven books and over 180 visionary female authors to best-seller status. Our powerful, high-visibility publishing, marketing, and list-building packages have brought these authors the positive, dynamic exposure they need to attract their ideal audience and thrive in their businesses.

Now, through our new hybrid publishing division, we're excited to offer the same proven feminine marketing model to individual authors. Our packages provide mission-driven authors, businesswomen, coaches, and personal development professionals with a voice and a venue to share their wisdom and expertise.

ILP's authors reap the benefits of being a part of a sacred family of inspirational multimedia brands which deliver the best in transformational and empowering content across a wide range of platforms. Our hybrid publishing packages provide visionary female authors with access to our proven best-seller model, high-profile multimedia exposure across all of Linda's imprints (including *Aspire Magazine*, the "Inspired Conversations" radio show on OM Times

Radio, the Inspired Living Giveaway, Inspired Living Secrets, and exposure to Linda's loyal personal audience of over 44,000 women and 22,000 social media followers).

If you are ready to publish your transformational book, or share your sacred story in one of ours, we invite you to join us!

Inspired Living Publishing ~ Transforming Women's Lives, One Story at a Time™

If you enjoyed this book, visit
www.InspiredLivingPublishing.com
and sign up for ILP's e-zine to receive news about hot new releases, promotions, and information on exciting author events.